The Bible Made Easy™: Hebrews

God's Last Will and Testament

Ann Moore

Fog (friends of God) Publishing Company
Houston

The Bible Made Easy™: Hebrews
—God's Last Will and Testament—

by Ann Moore

FOG (friends of God) Publishing Company/September 1995

"Jacob, listen, this is what the Lord, your creator, says—the One Who formed you, Israel, 'Don't be afraid; I have redeemed you. I have called you out by name and you belong to Me. When you pass through waters, I will be there with you—the rivers won't engulf you. When you walk through fire, you won't be seared or burned by its flame. That's because I am the *Lord your God*, the same *Holy One* of Israel and your *Saviour*. . . . You are a treasure to Me. . . . And I love you.'"
Isaiah 43:1-4 (paraphrased)

Printed in the United States of America
First U.S. edition

From the Desk of Ann Moore

Dear reader,

This is a difficult letter to write as it forces at least a minikin of acknowledgement of authorship. Though thousands of hours were spent researching, paraphrasing, reading, and writing, on the whole I do not see this as a work to which I can lay majority claim. Therefore Ann Moore, a pen name, was assigned by the publisher so that you, the reader, could reference the book by its author. At the same time the pen name allowed the anonymity sought for an inspired rather than authored work.

By inspired, I mean that I had no premise of my own, no agenda, not much of a thought toward discovery when I began the two years of research and paraphrasing of the *Letter to the Hebrews*. Compelled, nevertheless, to study and write, I would pray, "Dear God, let me be Your servant, give me the words." And He did. Looking back at some of the paraphrases, I know with certainty that there is no way I could have come up with these by myself.

Why Hebrews? I don't know. But by the end of this endeavor, I had of course developed a theory. That being that the *Letter to the Hebrews* is the bridge between the Old and New Testaments of the Bible. Not only because of its numerous references to Old Testament prophecy, but also because it is key to understanding why Christians and Jews are true brothers and why they may share in the promises of God to the faithful.

Why a paraphrase? Why now? My guess: in the present world that seems to be closing in on us while simultaneously out of our control, and in the future world wherein Bible prophecy seems to indicate both Christian and Jew will be persecuted, this brotherhood may be essential for survival of the followers of both faiths.

Ultimately, of course, it is not my theory or any other that explains why the original letter or this paraphrased and amplified work is important. Rather it is the work that God accomplishes in you, the reader, that gives each book its *raison d'être*.

The *Letter*'s original author (also of unknown identity) was obviously a Jew speaking to early Jewish (or "Hebrew") Christians whom the author was helping to understand the new covenant God had made for man through the life and death of Jesus. Extensively quoting from the *Psalms* and also from *Jeremiah* and *Habakkuk* the author grounded the audience, building the dissertation from a foundation of scriptures with which the audience was extremely familiar. That the quoted verses were considered prophetic in nature is inferred by the author's assumptive presentation of such as absolute and understood. They pertain to Christ as creator, King, beneficiary, representative and as having permanent dominion over all.

The author shows why Jesus had to suffer and die to fulfill God's plan for mankind; contrasts God's old will with His new one; and puts into perspective the Mosaic Law, sacrifices and the priesthood. Symbolism of earthly things, the dwelling place of God, and God's guaranteed promises are explained in detail. The *Letter* encouraged the Hebrew Christians to be faithful to the teachings of the holy scriptures and the teachings of Jesus passed down through the early church leaders so as to obtain the promised inheritance.

It's true most Bibles use the word *covenant* where I have substituted *will and testament*. However, that the author used the word *covenant* in the same way we might use *will* is clearly evident in Chapter 9:16 and 17. In those verses the author states: "Where there is a covenant, the one who makes it has to die. It's of course never in effect while the one who made it lives, since a covenant is only valid when death occurs."

So now we can read the *Letter to the Hebrews* from an unusual vantage point—as intended heirs under God's last will and testament. What a concept. But it's not mine. I'm just a servant and an heir. That's exciting enough for me. Hope you come away with the same feeling as I did after analyzing this incredible book of the Bible from a little different perspective.

I thank God that He allowed me to serve Him by refreshing the message of this important letter to the early Christian Hebrews. So, though it may be picked apart like fried chicken at a southern summer picnic and criticized through the tightly focused eyes of the ones with all the answers, I am certain that God will keep His promise that His Word will not return to Him void. Those of you affected by this book, may God richly bless your life. Praise Him daily and ask Him how you can serve Him. The answer may surprise you.

Ann Moore

How to Use This Book

The Bible Made Easy: Hebrews – God's Last Will and Testament is an easy-to-read paraphrase of the Bible's *Letter to the Hebrews* and may therefore be read and enjoyed simply as a devotional, enhanced by a thorough index of names, places and Biblical concepts.

The book also lends itself to an in-depth personal or group Bible study. Each page contains one verse of the Hebrews text, extensively supported by scriptures from the Old Testament, which foreshadow Christ's mission on earth, and the New Testament, which depict the impact of His mission on both Jew and Gentile.

On the outer corner of each page, top and bottom, find chapter and verse references. Where two or more complete thoughts coincide in one verse, and where the author found supporting scripture references for those thoughts, the verse was divided into subsections a.,b.,c. and so forth.

A drop cap indicates the beginning of a verse or subsection of a verse. No drop cap at the beginning of a page indicates the verse was started on a prior page and continued onto that page.

The paraphrased Hebrews verses are at the top portion of each page. Separated from the Hebrews verses by a gothic border, the reference verses (also paraphrased) occupy the lower portion of a page. Sometimes the reference verses carry over several pages, after the verse is already completed.

Brackets [ ] are used by the author, Ann Moore, to indicate her own amplified interpretation or clarification of the meaning of the original author. Parentheses ( ) are used to indicate an implied meaning in the original work. Moore considered a meaning to be implied if the original author had previously made reference to the concept.

The Chapter Outline in the front pages of the book and the extensive Index in the back were designed to be useable tools for study and devotion. Both are keyed to page numbers.

If you have any suggestions for the use of this book, corrections or comments, please write us so that we may consider such when printing future editions. Thank you.

FOG (friends of God) Publishing Company

Chapter Outline

Chapter Outline

Chapter Outline

FOG (friends of God) Publishing Company

 od spoke to the fathers,

[Fathers of the Jewish Faith: Moses and Abraham]

<u>To Moses</u>

John 9:29 We know that God spoke to Moses. . . .

Hebrews 3:5 Moses was faithful to God, as a servant giving testimony to God's words.

<u>To Abraham</u>

Genesis 21:12 But God said to Abraham, "Don't be stressed over the boy and your maid; listen to what Sarah says because your descendants shall be named after Isaac." [Note: God later gave Isaac's son, Jacob, an alternative name, *Israel*, by which the descendants were called, thus fulfilling God's command.]

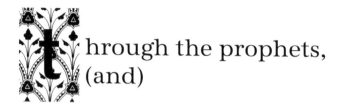

hrough the prophets, (and)

Acts 3:20,21 . . . [Then the Lord will] send Jesus, the Messiah appointed for you, Who must stay in heaven until God restores all things, just as God spoke by the *mouth of His holy prophets* from ancient time.

<u>David called a prophet</u>

Acts 2:29,30,31 Brothers, I tell you with confidence with regard to the patriarch, David, that he died and was buried. His tomb is a witness today. Knowing that God had sworn an oath to him to seat *one* of his descendants upon his throne, *because he was a prophet*, he saw in the future and spoke of Christ's resurrection.

 ost recently He has spoken to us through his Son,

 **W**hom He appointed the inheritor of all things,

Psalm 2:8 "Just ask Me, and I will absolutely give the nations as Your *inheritance,* and everything in and of the earth as Your possession."

Matthew 28:18 And Jesus came up [to the disciples, after His resurrection] and said to them, "I have been *given* all authority in heaven and on earth."

Mark 12:7 <u>Jesus's parable</u> "But these vine-growers said to each other, 'This is the *heir*; let's go kill him; then his inheritance will be ours.'"

Romans 8:16,17 The Spirit Himself testifies with our spirit that we are God's children. Now, if we are His children, then that makes us God's heirs also, *heirs along with Christ* (if we suffer with Christ, [it's] so we may be given glory with Him).

hrough Whom He also created the world.

John 1:1-3 The Word was in the beginning of all things. The Word was with God. The Word was, in fact, God. He was *with God* from the first. All things came to exist *through Him.* There is nothing in existence that began without Him.

Hebrews 11:3 By faith we understand that the worlds were *created by the Word* of God (Christ), so that what we see is made from things we can't see.

II Peter 3:5 They are willfully ignorant of the fact that by the *Word* of God the heavens existed a long time ago and that the earth was formed by and out of water.

Genesis 1:2,6 The earth was shapeless and void [of life] and darkness was over the deep surface. The *Spirit of God* was moving over the waters' surface. Then God said, "Let there be an expanse of earth in the middle of the waters and let it separate one body of water from another."

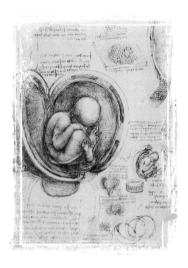

John 1:10 He (Christ) was in the world, and the *world was made through Him*, yet the world did not know [their own Creator].

I Corinthians 8:6 For us there is only one God, Who we call "Father", and everything came *from* Him, and we exist for God. Also (there is only) one Lord Jesus Christ, and everything came *through* Him, and we exist *through* Christ.

Colossians 1:16 In Christ, all things in heaven and all things on earth were created, both the visible and the invisible. The seat of sovereign power, the power to rule, the law and its enforcement, both in the invisible heavenly [hierarchy] and here on earth–*all things* have been created *through* Christ and *for* Christ.

Romans 11:36 All things are from Christ, *through Christ* and for Christ. Glorify Him through the ages. Amen.

Hebrews 2:10 In bringing many sons to glory, it was fitting for Christ to perfect Himself as man's Saviour through sufferings, as *all things* are made *for* Christ and made *through* Christ.

Philippians 2:6,7 Christ did not claim equality with God, though He existed in the form of God [as He thought it would be beyond human comprehension]. Instead, He acted as a bonded servant [or slave] [to God], taking on the attributes of men and setting His privileges aside. [Note: implicit in the verb *grasped*, used in several Bible translations for this verse, are the ideas of "laying claim to" and "intellectual comprehension"–both meanings, as used here, give a fuller understanding of Christ's action of laying aside His divinity.]

John 17:5 Jesus speaking to God, the Father "And now, glorify Me together with Yourself, Father, with the glory which I always had with You before the world was in existence."

John 8:58 Jesus said to them, "With absolute truth, I tell you: before Abraham came into being, *I AM.*" [Note: "I AM" is one of the names God calls Himself–Exodus 3:14]

John 17:24 <u>Jesus praying</u> "Father, I desire that they, whom You gave to Me, be with Me where I am, so they may behold My glory bestowed by You; for You have loved Me *before the foundation of the world* was laid."

Matthew 25:34 Then the King (the Son of Man–vs 31) will say to (the sheep) on His right, "You, who are blessed [to know] My Father, come here; *inherit* the kingdom [We] have been preparing for you since [We] started creating *the world.*"

Revelation 13:8 All those who live on earth will worship (the beast), that is everyone whose name has not been *written from the foundation of the world* in the book of life of the Lamb [the Christ] Who has been killed.

Revelation 17:8 "The beast that you saw existed and then didn't, but is about to come up out of the deep and go to destruction. When they see the beast come back who existed once, those who live on earth will wonder whose name has not been written in the book of life *since the foundation of the world.*"

Psalm 102:25 "*You founded the earth* long ago, and the heavens were created by Your hands."

Isaiah 48:16 <u>Isaiah prophesying Christ speaking</u> "Come close to Me and listen: from the beginning I have never spoken secretly, *from the beginning of creation, I was there.* And now, the Lord God (YHWH) has sent Me and His Spirit."

Jesus is the exact representation of God's nature and holds all things together by the power of His Word.

II Corinthians 4:4 . . . [Satan,] the god of this world, has deceived the minds of the unbelieving so that they are blinded to the truth of the glory of Christ, Who Himself is the *image* of God.

John 1:1,2 The Word was in the beginning of all things. The Word was with God. The Word was, in fact, God.

John 1:14 And The Word came in the flesh. . . .

Psalm 12:6 The words of the Lord are pure words, pure as silver heated in the center of the earth seven times.

John 8:51 <u>Jesus speaking</u> "With absolute truth, I tell you: anyone of you who keeps My Word shall never die."

e made purification of sins.

Revelation 19:13,14 <u>John's prophetic vision of the Messiah</u> He has on a kingly robe; its corner is dipped in blood. His name is called *The Word of God.* The armies of heaven are following him.

Isaiah 53:5 <u>Isaiah prophesying about the Christ</u> He was wounded for our sins. He was put down and crushed due to *our* own imperfection. It fell upon Him to *purify us* for our own well-being, and by His being thrashed, we are healed.

Isaiah 53:6 He took on the discipline meant for us. We were the ones that went our own way, wandering off from God, but He took our guilt all on Himself.

Deuteronomy 32:43 Rejoice, O nations, along with His people, for He will avenge the blood of His [dead] servants, and will render vengeance on those who oppose Him, and will *pay the sacrifice* to make amends for His land and His own people.

He sat down at God's right.

Ephesians 1: 20,21 "... He raised Him from the dead and seated Him at His right hand [the highest place of honor] in the heavenly places, far above all (government) rule and authority and power and spheres of authority and (far above) every name that is named—not only in this day and time, but also in the age to come."

Mark 16:19 After the Lord Jesus had spoken (to his eleven disciples), He was received by heaven and sat down at God's right hand.

<u>David prophesying regarding the Christ</u>

Psalm 110:1 The Lord (YHWH) says to my Lord: "Sit at My *right hand,* until I make Your enemies a footstool for Your feet."

Psalm 110:5 The Lord is Your right hand. In the day of His great anger He'll destroy kings and break their kingdoms.

 e had become much better than the angels; His inheritance is better.

Psalm 2:8 <u>God speaking regarding the Christ</u> ". . . I will absolutely give the nations as Your inheritance, and everything in and of the earth as Your possession."

Psalm 45:7 <u>Prophesy regarding the Christ</u> "Because You loved what is right to God and hated wickedness, Your God has anointed You [King], above Your comrades, with the (anointing) oil of joy.

ou know He never said to any angel: "Today I have conceived You"; or

—Psalm 2:7

Psalm 2:1-12 <u>David prophesying regarding the Christ and Christ's reign</u> Why are the gentile countries in an uproar and their people scheming in vain? The kings of the earth are set in their position, and the governments advise each other [to oppose] the Lord (YHWH) and against his anointed [Messiah], saying: "Let's break their binding chains apart and rid ourselves of the strings that attach us to Them!" But the Lord, sitting in the heavens, laughs at them, scoffs at them. Then [God] will speak through His anger and terrify them with His furious rage: "But as for Me, I have installed My King upon Zion, the nation I set apart for Myself." [And the Christ said,] "I will surely tell of the Lord's proclamation [decree]: He said to Me, '*You are My Son; today I have begotten You.* Just ask Me, and I will absolutely give the nations as Your inheritance, and everything in and of the earth as Your possession. You shall break these peoples with a rod of iron. You shall shatter them like (broken) dishes and pottery.'" Now, therefore, kings and governments, show some understanding and discretion.

"I will be His Father, and He shall be My Son."

—2 Samuel 7:14

You who by your actions are judging the earth, this is your warning: worship the Lord (YHWH) with reverence and rejoice while yet trembling. Bow down and be humble to the Son, in case, otherwise, He becomes angry, and you die in the way; for His righteous anger may soon be ignited. How blessed are all who take refuge in Him (the Son).

II Samuel 7:12-16 <u>God to David through Nathan, the prophet</u> "When your days are complete and you rest in your grave, I will raise up your descendant after you, Who will come forth from you, and I will establish His kingdom. He shall build a house for My name, and I will establish the throne of His kingdom forever. *I will be a Father to Him and He will be a Son to Me.* When He commits iniquity, I will correct Him with the rod of men and the strokes of the sons of men, but My loving kindness shall not depart from Him. . . . Your house and your kingdom shall endure before Me forever; your throne shall be established forever."

Matthew 3:16,17 . . . (John the Baptist) saw the Spirit of God descending like a dove upon (Jesus), and a voice from heaven said, *"This is My beloved Son*, with Whom I am very pleased."

Mark 9:7 Then a cloud came up and covered them (Jesus, Moses, and Elijah), and a voice came out of the cloud: *"This is My beloved Son*; listen to Him!"

Revelation 21:7 <u>Christ speaking on His throne</u> "The one who overcomes shall inherit these things. *I will be his God and he will be My son."*

Hosea 1:10 . . . And a time will come when in the same place where (God) said to the sons of Israel, "You are not My people," (He) will say to them, "You are the sons of the living God."

When He brought this firstborn into the world, He said, "Let all the angels of God worship Him."

Psalm 97:7 . . . All you gods worship Him.

Isaiah 45:23 "I have sworn by Myself, in righteousness, and I will not go back on My own Word, that every knee will bow to Me, every tongue will swear allegiance to Me."

Isaiah 24:21-23 In that day, the Lord (YHWH) will punish the angels and the rulers of the earth. They will be herded together like prisoners in prison and there they will be confined. After many days, they will be punished. Then the moon will not show, nor the sun; for the Lord of hosts will reign on Mount Zion and in Jerusalem, and will be glorious.

Revelation 7:11,12 All the angels were standing around the throne. . . . Then they fell on their faces before it and worshiped God, saying, "Amen, may our God have blessing and glory, wisdom and thanksgiving, honor and power and might forever and ever. Amen."

Revelation 11:15-17 . . . There suddenly were loud voices in heaven: "The whole world has become the kingdom of our Lord and of His Christ; and He will reign forever and ever." And the twenty-four elders, sitting on their thrones before God, fell on their faces and worshiped Him: "Thank you, O Lord God, Almighty, Who is and always has been. You have taken Your great power and have begun to reign."

Revelation 19:10 I fell to (the angel's) feet to worship him, and he said, "Don't do that. *I am a fellow servant* with you and your brothers who hold the testimony of Jesus—that is the spirit of prophecy. Worship God."

Revelation 22:8,9 I am John, the one who heard and saw this vision. When I did, I fell to worship at the feet of the angel who showed me this vision. The *angel said* to me, "Don't do that; *I am a fellow servant* along with you and your brothers the prophets and with anyone who heeds the words of this book. Worship God."

Of the angels He says:
"Who (but Me) makes
His angels like winds
and (the angels) that minister
to Him like flames of fire."

Psalm 104:4 He (God) makes the winds His messengers and flaming fire His ministers. [Note: the word "angel" derives from "messenger".]

Mark 8:38 <u>Jesus speaking</u> "Whoever is ashamed of Me and of My Words in this adulterous age, the Son of Man will likewise be ashamed of him when He comes in the glory from His Father *with the holy angels.*"

Revelation 10:1 I saw another strong angel coming down out of the heavens, girded by a cloud; there was a rainbow of light and color around his head, his face was as bright as the sun, and his feet like *columns of fire.*

Revelation 14:6,7 I saw another angel *flying in midheaven*, preaching an eternal gospel to all those living on earth: "Fear God, give Him glory, the hour of His judgment has come. Worship Him who made the heaven, earth, sea, and springs of waters."

Of the Son He says: "Your throne, O God is forever; the righteous scepter is Your scepter of Your kingdom.

Psalm 45:6-7 Your throne, O God, is forever and ever; a scepter of uprightness is the scepter of Your kingdom. You have loved what is right to God and hated wickedness; Your God, has anointed You [King], above Your comrades, with the (anointing) oil of joy.

Psalm 9:7 The Lord (YHWH) lives on forever; He has installed His throne for judgment.

Psalm 22:27,28 All the earth will remember and turn to the Lord (YHWH); the families of all the countries will worship before You. The kingdom belongs to the Lord (YHWH); He rules over the nations.

Daniel 7:13,14 . . . The Son of Man was presented before the ancient of days [God] and was given glory and rule over a kingdom. . . . His control will last forever. His kingdom won't be destroyed.

ou have loved goodness and hated lawlessness, therefore God has anointed You with the oil of joy above Your peers."

Psalm 45:7 <u>Prophesy regarding the Christ</u> Because You loved what is right to God and hated wickedness, Your God has anointed You [King], above Your comrades, with the (anointing) oil of joy.

Romans 7:12,14 The Law is holy; the commandments are holy and totally good. . . . The Law is spiritual. . . .

John 15:11 <u>Jesus speaking</u> "I have said these things to you so that you may experience My joy and, therefore, be full of joy."

John 16:20 <u>Jesus speaking</u> "With absolute truth I tell you that you will weep and be sorry, but the world will rejoice. You will be sorrowful, but your sadness will be changed to *joy*."

And (of the Son he also says:) "You, Lord, in the beginning laid the foundation of the earth. You created the heavens with Your own hands. They will both perish, but *You will remain.*

[The writer of the Letter to the Hebrews, a Christian-Jew himself, interprets this passage as the prophet-king David speaking of Christ, rather than God the Father, laying the foundations of the earth. *Compare to references on pages 17-21, pertaining to Christ creating the world.*]

Isaiah 24:3-6 Isaiah prophesying The earth will be completely wasted, completely spoiled, for the Lord has spoken His Word. The earth sadly withers and fades. The exalted people of the world fade away. The earth is polluted by its inhabitants. They break laws and ordinances and they broke their everlasting agreement with God [to take care of the earth—Genesis 1:28]. Therefore the earth is cursed through its guilty inhabitants. Therefore the inhabitants of the earth are burned, except for a few.

All of them will wear out like a garment; they will be changed like clothing; and You will roll them up as an overcoat. But You are always the *same* and You *will live forever.*" —*Psalm 102:25-27*

Isaiah 51:6 "Look up at the sky, then down at the earth. The sky will vanish like a puff of smoke. The earth will wear out like a garment. And earth's inhabitants will die likewise. But My salvation shall be forever. My goodness shall never be lessened."

Revelation 21:1 I saw a new heaven and earth. The first heaven and the first earth died. There wasn't any sea at all [in the new earth].

Revelation 22:13,14 "I am the Alpha and Omega; the first, the last; the beginning and the end." Those who cleanse themselves are blessed in that they will have the right to the tree of life and to enter the (holy) city [*new Jerusalem*].

Revelation 22:5 There won't be a need for night. They won't need a lamp for light, not even the sun, because the Lord God will shed light on them, and they (Christ's servants) shall reign forever and ever.

Daniel 7:13,14 . . . The Son of Man was presented before the ancient of days [God] and was given glory and rule over a kingdom. All the people of all the countries were to serve Him. His control will last forever. His kingdom won't be destroyed.

But to what angel has He ever said: "Sit at My right hand until I put Your enemies under Your feet"?

Psalm 110:1-3,5-7 <u>David prophesying about the Messiah</u> The Lord (YHWH) says to my Lord, "Sit at My *right hand,* until I make Your enemies a footstool for Your feet." The Lord (YHWH) will stretch forward Your strong scepter from Zion, saying, "Rule in the middle of Your enemies." Your people will volunteer freely in the day of Your power. In holy array, Your youths surface like the dew born of dawn. The Lord is Your right hand; in the day of His great anger He destroys kings and breaks their kingdoms. He will sentence certain nations and fill them with death. He will rout the commanders-in-chief over a broad country and drink from their brook. His head will be held high.

Revelation 3:21 <u>Christ telling John what to write</u> "I will grant to the one who overcomes the right to sit down with Me on My throne, since I also overcame and sat down with My Father on His throne."

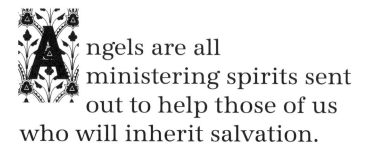 ngels are all
ministering spirits sent
out to help those of us
who will inherit salvation.

Psalm 103:20 You, His angels, mighty and strong, *performing His Word*, obeying the Voice of His Word!, bless the Lord (YHWH).

Daniel 7:10 A flowing river of fire was coming out in front of Him, thousands upon thousands *were attending Him*, and myriads upon myriads were standing in front of Him. The court sat, then the books were opened.

Matthew 4:6 <u>Devil tempting Jesus quoting from Psalm 91:11-12</u> "If You are the Son of God then throw Yourself down; after all, it's written in scripture: 'He will *charge His angels* with all concerning You; they will hold You up with their hands so that You won't even stub Your toe on a stone and stumble.'"

Luke 22:44 In agony, he prayed feverishly, and His sweat became like drops of blood, falling down to the ground.

 ay close attention so that we won't drift away from what we've heard.

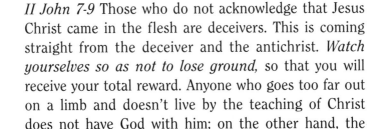

II John 7-9 Those who do not acknowledge that Jesus Christ came in the flesh are deceivers. This is coming straight from the deceiver and the antichrist. *Watch yourselves so as not to lose ground,* so that you will receive your total reward. Anyone who goes too far out on a limb and doesn't live by the teaching of Christ does not have God with him; on the other hand, the person who lives by the teaching has both the Father and the Son with him.

II Peter 3:17 Be on guard, beloved brothers and sisters in Christ, *so you don't fail in keeping the faith* by being swayed by the error of men with no principles.

or if what has been
spoken through angels
has proven unchangeable,

Acts 7:38,53 <u>Stephen's defense—here he is referring to Moses</u> "This is the one who was with our ancestors in the synagogue in the wilderness, along with the angel who was speaking to him on Mount Sinai. He received living oracles to pass on to . . . you who received the law as ordained by angels, but still did not keep it."

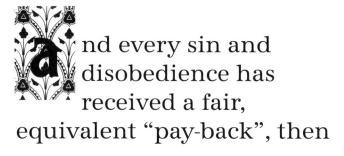

nd every sin and disobedience has received a fair, equivalent "pay-back", then

Hebrews 10:28 Anyone who willfully ignored the Law of Moses died with no mercy based on testimony from two or three witnesses.

Deuteronomy 17:2-6 "If there is found in any of your towns which the Lord your God has given you, a man or a woman who does what is evil in the sight of the Lord your God by transgressing His covenant, and has gone and served other gods and worshiped them, or the sun or the moon or any of the heavenly host, which I have not commanded; and if you're told or you hear about it, then you shall inquire thoroughly. And if it is true and absolutely certain that this detestable thing has been done in Israel, then you shall bring out that man or that woman who has done this evil thing to your gates and you shall stone them to death. On the evidence of two witnesses or three witnesses, that person shall be put to death; he shall not be put to death on the evidence of one witness."

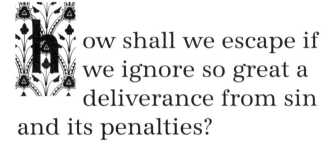 ow shall we escape if we ignore so great a deliverance from sin and its penalties?

Hebrews 10:29 How much more severe do you think the punishment will be for the person who treats the son of God like dirt and regards the blood of Jesus that validated His inheritance with God as impure and, further, has insulted the Holy Spirit of Grace?

Hebrews 12:25 Be sure that you don't refuse God Who speaks [to you]. Because if those who were warned by the prophets didn't escape, how much less chance shall we have to escape God Himself Who warns [us] from heaven?

Christ spoke the Word of salvation first, and it was confirmed to Paul and others by those who heard Him speak.

Luke 1:2 . . . Those who from the beginning were eyewitnesses and servants of the Word have handed down (their eyewitness accounts) to us.

Mark 16:19,20 After the Lord Jesus had spoken (to His eleven disciples), He was received by heaven and sat down at God's right hand. And they went out and preached everywhere, and the Lord was working with them, confirming the Word with signs.

God provided proof of this to them with signs, miracles, works of power, and distributions of the Holy Spirit,

John 4:48 "Unless you people see signs and wonders, you simply will not believe, will you?" Jesus asked him.

Mark 6:13 And they were casting out many demonic spirits and were anointing many sick people with oil and healing them.

I Corinthians 12:4,11 Now there are any number of gifts, but one and only one Holy Spirit Who distributes them.

Romans 12:6 Since our gifts differ according to the divine function given to us, let's each exercise them accordingly. . . .

ccording to His will.

Ephesians 1:5 We were predestined to be adopted as His sons through Jesus Christ, according to the kind intention of His will.

 od did not make the inhabited earth subject to the angels.

But testimonial is written that says: "What is man that You take thought of him? And the Son of Man that You care for Him?" —*Psalm 8:4*

Mark 11:27-30,32 . . . As (Jesus) was walking in the temple, the chief priests, scribes, and elders came up to Him and demanded, "By what authority are You doing these things? Who gave You this authority?" Jesus said, "Answer this one question, and then I'll tell you: was the baptism of John from heaven or from men?" . . . For all considered John to have been a prophet for sure.

John 16:15 Jesus speaking of the Holy Spirit [Spirit of Truth—vs 13] "All things that the Father has are Mine; therefore, He shall take what is Mine and reveal it to you."

Matthew 28:18 And Jesus came up [to the disciples, after His resurrection] and said to them, "I have been *given* all authority in heaven and on earth."

Yet You have made Him a little lower than the 'Elohim' [God's angels] and have given Him authority over everything You ever made.

—Psalm 8:5

John 17:2 <u>Jesus praying to God regarding Himself, "The Son"–vs 1</u>] "You have given Him authority over all mankind so that He may give eternal life to all whom You have given Him."

Luke 10:22 [Authority for] all things [has] been handed over to Me by My Father. No one really knows the Son except the Father, nor really knows the Father, except the Son, and anyone to whom the Son wishes to reveal Him.

You (God) made everything (Christ's) subject, putting all under His feet"—everything, nothing left out, even though it's not that way right now.

—Psalm 8:6

Psalm 110:1 <u>David prophesying regarding the Christ</u>
The Lord (YHWH) says to my Lord: "Sit at My *right hand,* until I make Your enemies a footstool for Your feet."

Psalm 22:28 The kingdom belongs to the Lord (YHWH) and He governs over the nations.

Daniel 7:14 (The Son of Man) was given glory and rule over a kingdom. . . . His control will last forever. His kingdom will not be destroyed.

John 12:48 "The one who rejects Me or the one who hears my new word and doesn't keep it, I don't judge him. I came to save the world, not judge it. (My Word will judge it in the last epoch.)"

Isaiah 9:6,7 A child will be born to us, a son will be given to us. The government will be His responsibility. He will be called "Wonderful Counselor", and "Mighty

God", "Eternal Father", and also "Prince of Peace". There will be no end to the increase of His Government or the increase of Peace. . . . The zeal of the Lord of angels will accomplish this.

By God's grace to us, Christ was made, for a little while, lower than "Elohim" [God's angels] so He could experience death for everyone.

Jesus speaking

John 8:51,52 "With absolute truth I tell you: anyone of you who keeps My Word shall never die."

John 17:19 "For their sakes I purify Myself, that they also may be pure in Truth."

John 15:13 "There is no greater love than to die for the sake of your friends."

John 3:16 "God loved the peoples of the earth so much that He gave us the only Son He ever conceived, so that whoever put faith in His Son wouldn't die, but, instead, live forever."

John 3:36 "The one who has faith in the Son shall live forever; but the one who does not obey the Son shall not live and, instead, incur God's lasting wrath."

John 6:40 "The will of My Father is that everyone who looks upon the Son and believes in Him should live forever; and that I Myself will elevate that one [to glory] on the last [epoch] day."

John 11:25,26 "I am the resurrection and the life [as spoken in prophecy]; even those who die shall live if they put faith in Me, and all those who live (having faith in Me) shall never see death." [Note: Read Hebrews 3:11-4:6 elaborating on God's tranquil rest and God's peace guaranteed to the faithful.]

Christ was crowned with glory and honor because of the suffering of death.

John 17:1,5,10 These things were spoken by Jesus Who, lifting His eyes up to heaven, said, "Father, the hour has come; glorify Your Son so that the Son may glorify You. . . . And now, glorify Me together with Yourself, Father, with the glory which I always had with You before the world came into existence. . . . All things that are Mine are Yours, and all that are Yours are Mine; and I have been magnified with glory in them."

Acts 3:13 The God of Abraham, Isaac, and Jacob—our own fathers—has magnified with glory His Servant, Jesus, the very One Whom you disowned in Pilate's presence (although Pilate wished to release Him) and thereby delivered Him [to His death].

I Peter 1:20,21 For His name and destiny were known before the foundation of the world, but He appeared at the end times for the sake of you who through Him are believers in God. God raised Him from the dead and gave Him glory, to give you faith and hope in God.

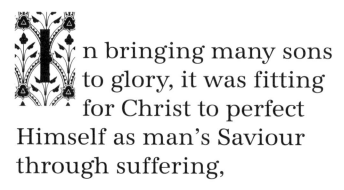

n bringing many sons to glory, it was fitting for Christ to perfect Himself as man's Saviour through suffering,

Hebrews 2:14 Suffering was a fitting means of Christ's perfection because we shared in the same flesh and blood. Through death he made Satan, who has the power over death, powerless.

as all things are made for Christ and made through Christ.

Romans 11:36 All things are from Christ, *through Christ,* and for Christ. Glorify Him through the ages. Amen.

Colossians 1:16 In Christ, all things in heaven and all things on earth were created, both the visible and the invisible. The seat of sovereign power, the power to rule, the law and its enforcement, both in the invisible heavenly [hierarchy] and here on earth—*all things* have been created *through* Christ and *for* Christ.

John 1:1-3 The Word was in the beginning of all things. The Word was with God. The Word was, in fact, God. He was *with God* from the first. All things came to exist *through Him.* There is nothing in existence that began without Him.

For both those of us who are purified and Christ, Who makes us pure, are all of one Father. This is why Christ unashamedly refers to us as "Brethren [or Brothers]".

John 17:11,12 Jesus praying "It's I Who am coming to you. I am no longer a part of the world, but they are. Holy Father, maintain them in Your name—the name you gave Me—so that they will be a union just as You and I are. I was keeping them in the name You gave Me while I was with them ["Jesus"] and I also guarded them. Not one was lost except the son of hell [Judas Iscariot], so the scripture prophecy would be fulfilled."

As David sang in the Scriptures—"I will proclaim Your name to My Brethren. In the midst of the synagogue I praise You",

Psalm 22:22 <u>David Speaking</u> I will tell of Your name to my brethren; I will praise You in the middle of the congregation.

Isaiah 8:17 I will wait for the Lord (YHWH) Who is hiding His face [right now] from Israel; I will be eagerly looking for Him, as a matter of fact.

Isaiah 25:9 <u>Prophesying about when God removes death and sadness from earth</u> In that day people will say: "Look, this is our God Whom we have waited for, so He might save us. This is the Lord (YHWH) for Whom we have been waiting! Let's celebrate His salvation."

and again, "I will put my trust in Him", and again, "Look at us, Me and the children whom God has given Me."

Isaiah 8:18 <u>About Isaiah, also Jesus, the suffering servant</u> I, and the children whom God has given me, perform signs and miracles in Israel that are from the Lord of angels who stays on Mount Zion.

Suffering was a fitting means of Christ's perfection because we shared in the same flesh and blood.

Isaiah 50:6 <u>Prophesy: Messiah speaking</u> I gave My back to those who struck Me and My cheeks to the ones who plucked out My beard. I was spit upon and humiliated, but I didn't cover My face.

Isaiah 63:4-6 <u>Prophesying about the Christ</u> He bore our griefs, Himself, and carried our sorrows. We thought He was afflicted, stricken by God. But He was pierced through for our transgressions and crushed for our ungodliness. He took on the discipline meant for us, so we're healed by His flogging. We were the ones who went our own way, wandering away from God—but He took our guilt all on Himself.

John 1:14 [Refer also to verse 10] And the Word became flesh and lived among us, and we looked upon His glory—glory that could only come from the Father—that was full of grace and full of truth.

Mark 8:31 Christ began to teach them that the "Son of Man" must suffer . . . and be rejected . . . and be killed . . . and rise from death.

hrough death He made Satan, who has the power over death, powerless.

I John 3:8 The one who makes a habit of sin is in with the devil because the devil has sinned since the first. The Son of God appeared for the purpose of destroying the works of the devil.

I John 5:12 He who belongs to the Son has the life; he who does not belong to the Son of God does not have the life. [Note: "the life" refers to eternal life–vs 11.]

I John 5:18,19 We know that we are God's, yet the entire world is under the power of the evil one. . . . And the One Who was born of God holds us, so the evil one doesn't touch us.

John 12:31 <u>Jesus speaking</u> "Judgment is now upon the peoples of this earth; their ruler [Satan] shall be expelled now."

Isaiah 25:8,9 <u>Prophesying about the new age</u> He will put an end to death for all time. The Lord (YHWH) God will dry everyone's tears. The Jews' disgrace will be removed from all the earth because the Lord (YHWH) has said that He would do it. In that day people will say: "Look, this is our God Whom we have waited for, so He might save us. This is the Lord (YHWH) for Whom we have been waiting! Let's celebrate His salvation."

Revelation 1:17,18 When I saw Him, I fell at His feet like a dead man. He laid His right hand on me and said, "Don't be afraid; I'm the first and the last, and the Living One; I died, but now, see, I am alive forever, and I have the keys to death and hell."

Hosea 13:14 I will put up ransom to keep them safe from the power of hell and to keep them from death. Death, where are your thorns, O hell, where is your sting? . . .

II Timothy 1:10 <u>God's purpose for calling us [vs 9]</u> has been disclosed by the appearance of our Saviour Christ Jesus, Who put an end to death and taught us of the life of immortality through the gospel of truth.

I Corinthians 15:24-26 He must rule until He has put all of His enemies under His feet. After He has abolished all rule and all authority and power, the last enemy that will be abolished is death. Then comes the end when He delivers up the kingdom to the Father.

And [He] delivers those who have been enslaved all of their lives by the fear of death.

Romans 8:6 A mind set on the "here and now" life leads to death, but a mind set on the in-dwelling spirit of good leads to life and peace.

Isaiah 30:15,16 This is what the Lord God (YHWH), the Holy One of Israel says, "You shall be saved in repentance and rest, your strength is in quietness and trust, but you are not willing. Instead you say 'no, we're leaving now', and you flee fast. . . ."

Isaiah 45:21 "There is no other God besides Me. I am a good and perfect God and Saviour; there is none but Me."

od does not help the angels, yet He helps the offspring (seed) of Abraham.

Romans 4:16,14,15,13 So that the *promise may be certain to all the descendants, not just to those who are of the Law [the Jews] but also to those who are of the faith [the Christian Gentiles] of Abraham* (who is the father of us all). It is by faith along with grace that we become heirs. . . . If those who are of the Law only are heirs, then faith is useless and the promise is nullified, for the Law brings God's anger. But where there is not law, there can't be a violation of the Law. . . . The promise to Abraham or to his descendants that he would be heir of the world was not as a result of the Law, but as a result of the goodness of faith.

Romans 9:6-8 They are not all Israel who are descended from Israel; neither are they all God's children because they are Abraham's descendants. But it is not as though the Word of God has changed. Scriptures say "through Isaac your descendants will be named". In other words, it is the children of the promise who are regarded as descendants, not the children of the flesh who are children of God.

Hosea 2:23 "I will say to those who were not My people, 'You are My people!' And they will say, 'You, God, are my God!'"

Hosea 1:10 The sons of Israel will be as numerous as the sand of the sea, too numerous to measure. And a time will come when in the same place where (God) said to the sons of Israel, "You are not My people," (He) will say to them, "You are the sons of the living God."

hrist of necessity had to be like His brothers in God

Philippians 2:6,7 Christ did not claim equality with God, though He existed in the form of God [as He thought it would be beyond human comprehension]. Instead, He acted as a bonded servant [or, slave] [to God], taking on the attributes of men and setting His privileges aside. [Note: implicit in the verb *grasped*, used in several Bible translations for this verse, are the ideas of "laying claim to" and "intellectual comprehension"–both meanings, as used here, give a fuller understanding of Christ's action of laying aside His divinity.]

John 1:14 The Word came in the flesh and lived among us, and we looked upon His glory–glory that could only come from the Father–that was full of grace and full of truth.

Romans 8:3,4 The [Mosaic] Law could not save us from sins because we're weak. But God saved us anyway, sending His own Son in the likeness of sinful man as a sin offering. He put sin to death in the flesh, but the

requirement of the Law is fulfilled in us who walk [in the way of goodness and truth and faith] in accord with the Spirit of God.

Galatians 4:4,5 When the preordained time came, God sent out His Son, born of a woman, born under the Mosaic Law, so the Son might purchase those of us subject to death under the Law, so that we could be adopted as sons.

o that He could be a merciful and faithful high priest,

Hebrews 4:15 In fact we do have a high priest Who can sympathize with our weaknesses because He has been tempted Himself, just like us, and still He is sinless.

Hebrews 5:1,2 Every high priest is appointed by God on behalf of other men and women so that they can offer gifts to God and sacrifices for human sins. Being human, the high priest can deal gently with those who are ignorant or misdirected, because the high priest himself is weak in so many things.

o make atonement, or reconciliation, with God for the sins of the people.

Sin offering described in ancient scriptures

II Chronicles 29:24 The priest slaughtered them (the animal offerings) and purified the altar with their blood to atone for all of Israel. Upon orders from the king (Hezekiah), they burned the sin offering for all Israel.

Leviticus 4:24-26 "Laying his hand on the head of the male goat, he shall slay it in the same place where they slay the burnt offering before the Lord (YHWH); this is a sin offering. Then the priest is to take some of the blood of the sin offering with his finger and dab it on the horns of the altar for burnt offerings; the rest of the blood shall be poured out at the base of the altar for burnt offerings. In the case of the sacrifice of peace offerings, the priest shall offer all the animal's fat up in smoke on the altar. In this way, the priest shall make atonement for (the unintentional sinner), and the sinner shall be forgiven."

Messiah as a sin offering

Isaiah 53:10-12 The Lord (YHWH) was pleased to crush Him, putting Him to great sorrow. If He put Himself up as a guilt offering, He will see His children. He will extend His life, His hand will perform the pleasure of the Lord (YHWH). As a result of the suffering of His soul, He will see all this and be satisfied. The Righteous One, My Servant, will justify the many with His knowledge [of God and man], as He will bear the guilt of man's sins. Therefore, I will allot Him a portion with the great, and He will divide the takings with the mighty, because He gave of Himself even to death, being numbered with the sinners. He Himself bore the guilt of many and interceded for the real sinners.

Isaiah 53:6 He took on the discipline meant for us. We were the ones that went our own way, wandering off from God, but He took our guilt all on Himself.

Romans 5:10 If, while we were God's enemies, God made peace with us through the death of His Son, how much more so we shall be saved by His life now that peace has been made with God.

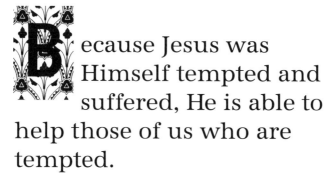

Because Jesus was Himself tempted and suffered, He is able to help those of us who are tempted.

Hebrews 4:15 In fact, we do have a high priest Who can sympathize with our weaknesses because He has been tempted, Himself, just like us, and still He is sinless.

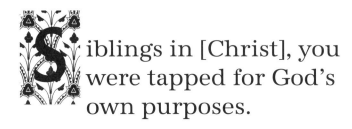

Siblings in [Christ], you were tapped for God's own purposes.

Hebrews 10:19,20 Therefore, brothers, we [should] have confidence to enter the holy place by the blood sacrifice of Jesus, by the new and living way initiated for us through the veil of His flesh.

Romans 11:29 The gifts of God and the calling of God [in this context to the Jews] cannot be revoked.

Romans 8:30 Those whom He predestined, He also called, He also justified, and He also glorified.

Romans 9:24 He didn't call us just from the Jews, but He called us from the Gentiles as well.

I Corinthians 1:9 God is faithful and called you into fellowship with His Son, Jesus Christ our Lord.

II Thessalonians 2:14 For this reason He called you through our true accounts (or gospel), so that you may receive the glory of our Lord Jesus Christ.

hink about Jesus—He was sent by God to teach *and* be our high priest.

John 17:8 <u>Jesus praying</u> "The words which You gave Me I have given to them, and they received them and truly did understand that I came forth from You, and they believed that You did indeed send Me."

Hebrews 5:1,9,10 Every high priest is appointed by God on behalf of other men and women so they can offer gifts to God and sacrifices for human sins. . . . (Christ) was perfected by God and became the source of everlasting salvation for all who obey Him through suffering. He was, therefore, designated as a high priest according to the Order of Melchizedek [and in that role, sacrificed *Himself* for our sins].

He was faithful to God Who made Him and sent Him out for His purpose, just as Moses was faithful.

Jesus was faithful to his purpose

John 17:3,6 <u>Jesus praying</u> "And this is eternal life: that they may know You, the only true God, and Jesus Christ Whom You sent. *I manifested Your name to the men whom You gave Me* out of the world; Yours they were, You gave them to Me, and they have kept Your Word."

John 19:28 Knowing that *all things had already been accomplished,* and in order that the Scripture might be fulfilled, Jesus said, "I am thirsty."

Moses was faithful

Exodus 40:16 Thus Moses did everything according to what the Lord had commanded him.

Numbers 12:7 "My servant Moses . . . is the most faithful of all My sons of Israel. With him I speak mouth to mouth." [Note: rather than through a dream or vision–vs 6.]

 f course, Jesus is counted worthy of more glory than Moses. After all, He created Moses and the Jews.

II Corinthians 3:7-11 Considering that the ministry of death, engraved on tablets of stone, came with such glory that the sons of Israel could not look closely at Moses's old but shining face, [you know that] the ministry of the Holy Spirit has come with much greater glory. Indeed, if the ministry of condemnation has glory, then the ministry of godly purity and goodness is full of glory. The fading glory (of the ministry of death) is surpassed by the lasting glory (of the ministry of the Holy Spirit).

 od creates everything, even this body of believers.

Genesis 1:1 At the first, God created the heavens and the earth.

Psalm 95:6-8 Come, let's worship and bow down; let's kneel before the *Lord our Maker*. Now, He is our God, we are His People. We wander in His pasture and feed from His hand. Do not harden your hearts today if you hear His voice calling. . . .

Isaiah 44:1,2 "Listen up now, O Jacob, My servant and Israel, my chosen peoples: [I am] the Lord Who made you and formed you from the womb."

 oses was faithful to God as a servant giving testimony to God's Words.

Numbers 6:22-27 Then the Lord (YHWH) said to Moses, "Go speak to Aaron and to his sons and tell them this: 'This is the way you shall bless the sons of Israel.' Say 'The Lord bless you and keep you; the Lord make His face shine upon you and be gracious to you; the Lord lift up His countenance on you and give you peace.' That's how they shall call on My name on behalf of the sons of Israel and then I will bless them."

Numbers 1:1-3,17-19 Then the Lord (YHWH) spoke to Moses in the wilderness of the Sinai, in the meeting tent, on the first day of the second month in the second year after they had come out of the land of Egypt, saying, "Take a census of all the congregation of the sons of Israel by their families, by their fathers' households, according to the number of names, every male, a head count from twenty years old and upward, whoever is able to go out to war in Israel, you and Aaron number them by their armies." So Moses and

Aaron took these men according to their name and they assembled the entire congregation together on the first day of the second month. Then they registered by ancestry in their families, by their fathers' households, according to the number of names, from twenty years old and upward, a head count, just as the Lord had told Moses. So he numbered them in the wilderness of the Sinai.

Numbers 11:24 So Moses went out and told the people what the Lord had spoken.

Numbers 9:1,2,4 The Lord spoke to Moses in the wilderness of the Sinai, in the first month of the second year after they had come out of the land of Egypt, saying, "The sons of Israel shall observe the Passover at its appointed time." . . . *So Moses told the sons of Israel to observe the Passover.*

Numbers 8:5,6,20 The Lord spoke to Moses again, saying, "Select the Levites from the sons of Israel to cleanse them." . . . *Thus Moses and Aaron* and all the congregation of the sons of Israel *did* to the Levites *according to all that the Lord had commanded Moses concerning them.*

Deuteronomy 34:10-12 Since that time *no prophet has risen in Israel like Moses, whom the Lord knew face to face,* [accomplishing] all the signs and wonders in Egypt against Pharaoh, his servants, and the nations which the Lord sent him to perform, and all the mighty power and great terror which Moses performed in the sight of Israel.

**hrist was faithful as God's Son ministering to God's people.**

Matthew 3:17 . . . A voice from heaven said, "This is My beloved Son, with Whom I am very pleased."

Luke 3:22 The Holy Spirit, in bodily form like a dove, descended upon Him, and a voice came from heaven, "You are My beloved Son; I am very pleased with You."

Luke 22:15-20 (Jesus) said to them, "I wish very much to eat this Passover with you before I suffer because I shall never have it again until the kingdom of God is fulfilled." He took a cup and gave thanks and said, "Take this and pass it around among yourselves; I myself will not drink wine from now on until the kingdom of God comes." He took some bread and gave thanks, then broke it, and gave it to them, saying, "This is My body which I give up for you; do this to remember Me." Then He took the cup after they had eaten and said, "This cup represents My blood poured out for you that creates God's new will for mankind."

 s a body of believers, we belong to Christ

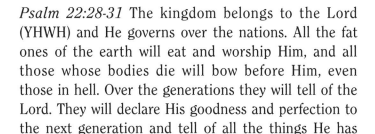

Psalm 22:28-31 The kingdom belongs to the Lord (YHWH) and He governs over the nations. All the fat ones of the earth will eat and worship Him, and all those whose bodies die will bow before Him, even those in hell. Over the generations they will tell of the Lord. They will declare His goodness and perfection to the next generation and tell of all the things He has done.

Isaiah 51:1 Hey, you people who want to be good, who seek the Lord, listen to me—look at whom and where you came from.

f we have lasting belief, faith, and hope.

Mark 11:24 <u>Jesus speaking</u> "I tell you, *believe that you have received all things for which you pray and ask* and you shall be granted your prayers."

<u>Isaiah prophesying about the children of Zion</u>

Isaiah 49:23 "Kings will be your guardians. Their commonwealths will nurse you. They will bow low to you with their faces to the ground and lick the dust off your feet. You will know I am the Lord (YHWH); *those who wait hopefully for Me will not be embarrassed.*"

Psalm 9:14 I wish to tell of Your praises, Lord. *I wish* to rejoice over Your salvation in the City of Zion.

L isten to what the Holy Spirit has said: "Today if you hear God's voice saying, 'Don't block Me out like they did when they tried Me in the wilderness;

—Psalm 95:7,8

Psalm 95:8 Do not harden your hearts today if you hear His voice calling like (they did) at Meribah, like the time of Massah in the wilderness.

Exodus 17:2-7 The people argued with Moses, "Give us water to drink." Moses said, "Why are you quarreling with me and testing the Lord (YHWH)?" But the people kept grumbling and started complaining about being brought all the way out into the wilderness just to die of thirst. Moses [in near-panic] cried out to God to help him, saying, "Much more, and they're going to stone me!" So God told Moses to go with some elders in front of the people to the rock of Horeb and to strike the rock with the same staff he used to strike the Nile. Moses did it and water came out, as God promised. But he named the place Massah and Meribah, meaning "Test and Quarrel".

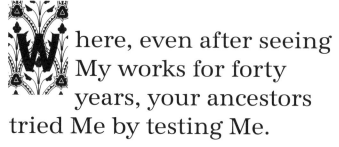

here, even after seeing My works for forty years, your ancestors tried Me by testing Me.

—Psalm 95:9

Psalm 95:9 <u>Referring to scripture, Numbers 14:22</u> Your fathers tested Me, they tried Me, although they had seen My work.

Numbers 14:22 <u>Lord (YHWH) to Moses</u> "All those men . . . saw My glory and My signs that I performed in Egypt and in the wilderness. . . . After all that, they have *put Me to the test ten times* and haven't even listened to My voice."

Numbers 14:11 The Lord (YHWH) said to Moses, "How long will these people reject Me? How long are they not going to believe in Me, even after seeing all the signs I have performed?"

I loathed that whole generation because I knew they would always forget Me in their heart and not follow My ways.

—Psalm 95:10

Psalm 95:10 <u>Referring to scripture, Numbers 3:14</u> "I loathed that generation for forty years and decided these people's hearts are not in the right place—they don't know Me or how I work."

Numbers 14:27 <u>Lord (YHWH) to Moses and Aaron</u> "How long should I put up with this evil congregation who are grumbling about Me? I have heard the complaints against Me made by the sons of Israel."

Numbers 14:30-32 <u>The Lord commanded Moses and Aaron to say this to all of Israel</u> "There is no way you're going to live in the land where I swore to settle you, no one except Caleb, the son of Jephunneh, and Joshua, the son of Nun. However, I will bring your children, who you said would become a prey, and they shall be in the land that you rejected. As for *you*, your *corpses shall fall in the wilderness.*"

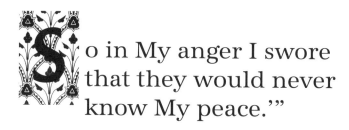

o in My anger I swore that they would never know My peace.'"

—Psalm 95:11

Psalm 95:11 "Therefore, I swore in My wrath, the truth is they shall not enter My rest."

Numbers 14:23 "(This generation of Israel) shall by no means see the land that I swore to give their ancestors, nor shall anyone who rejected Me see it."

Numbers 14:29,33-35 "Your corpses shall fall in this wilderness, even all your mustered men, from twenty years old up—the whole lot of them who grumbled against Me. Your sons shall be shepherds for forty years in the wilderness until your corpses rot there, and they shall suffer because of your unfaithfulness. The same number of days (forty) you spied out the land you shall pay for your sins one year (forty years); you shall know that it is I Who oppose you. I the Lord (YHWH) have spoken and I will definitely do this to all this evil congregation gathered against Me. In this wilderness *they shall be destroyed, and there they shall die.*"

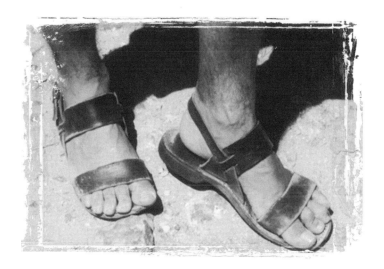

Deuteronomy 1:34,35 The Lord (YHWH) heard what you were saying and it made Him so angry that He took an oath, saying, "Not one of these men in this evil generation shall see the good land that I swore to give your fathers."

ake care, brothers, that none of you are evil or non-believing, falling away from the living God.

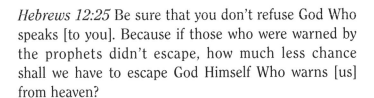

Hebrews 12:25 Be sure that you don't refuse God Who speaks [to you]. Because if those who were warned by the prophets didn't escape, how much less chance shall we have to escape God Himself Who warns [us] from heaven?

I Peter 1:13 Therefore, make your minds ready for action, keep your spirit sober, fix your hope completely on the kindness and forgiveness to be brought to you at the revelation of Jesus Christ.

All day long encourage each other, day after day, so that not one of you will be hardened by sinful tricks and lies.

I Peter 4:10,11 Since each one of you has received a special gift from God, use it in serving each other, as good fiduciaries of the encompassing kindness of God. Whoever speaks, speak the words of God; whoever serves, do so with the strength supplied by God, so that in all things God may be glorified through Jesus Christ, to Whom belongs glory and control for all time.

or we are in Christ's blessings if we keep our faith to the end.

I Peter 3:15 Make Christ your Lord in your hearts, always being ready to make a defense to every one who asks you why you have so much hope, but do this with gentleness and with reverence [for Christ].

I Peter 5:9,10 Resist (Satan), firm in your faith, realizing that your siblings in Christ the world over suffer the same experiences. After you have suffered for a little while, the God of all forgiveness, Himself, Who tapped you to receive everlasting glory with Christ, will make you perfect. He removes all elements of doubt; He will make you strong.

I John 2:17 . . . The inhabited earth is dying as are the cravings [of man]; but the one who follows God's will lives forever.

II Corinthians 11:3 I fear that just as the serpent deceived Eve with his cleverness, your minds might also be diverted from the pure simplicity of devotion to Christ.

Jude 20,21 Keep yourselves in the love of God, you beloved, building yourselves up in your faith, praying in the Holy Spirit, and wait anxiously for the forgiveness of our Lord Jesus Christ for eternal life.

Regarding the Words, "Do not harden your hearts, as when they provoked Me": who did make Him angry? Wasn't it all who were led by Moses out of Egypt?

[The Hebrews author is referencing again the scripture in Psalms and, in asking us these questions, is leading us to his conclusion in vs 19.]

And with whom was He angry for forty years? Wasn't it the sinners, whom He let die in the wilderness? And wasn't it the disobedient people that He swore He wouldn't let enter His peace?

In other words, it's obvious that they were not able to come into His peace because of their unbelief.

John 3:36 The one who has faith in the Son shall live forever, but the one who *does not obey* the Son shall not live, and instead incur God's lasting wrath.

Acts 13:39 "Through (Christ), everyone of you who *believes* is freed from all things by which you were enslaved under the Law of Moses."

Acts 13:41 <u>Reference to Habakkuk 1:5, the oracle seen by the prophet</u> 'You who scoff: look, marvel and then die, because I will accomplish work in your days that even if you were told, you would never believe.'

Even though a promise remains of entering God's tranquil rest—not death—let's be prudent so no one misses out on it.

Revelation 14:12,13 In this is the perseverance of the true believers who keep the commandments of God and keep their faith in Jesus: a voice from heaven said, "Write: 'Blessed are the dead who die in the Lord from now on!'" "Yes," said the Spirit, "they may take a rest from their labors because their deeds follow after them."

Revelation 2:7 'Let anyone who has an ear hear what the Spirit says to the churches: to the one who overcomes, I will grant you to eat from the tree of life, which is in the Paradise of God.'

Of course, we've had good news preached to us too, just as they did, but they didn't benefit from what they heard, because they did not have faith to go along with it.

I Thessalonians 2:13 We thank God all the time that when you received the Word of God's message from us, you accepted it, not as the word of men, but for what it actually is: the Word of God that accomplishes Its own work in those of you who believe.

I Thessalonians 1:9;2:1 They themselves report about us and our reception by you, and how you turned away from idols so as to serve the true, living God. *Our coming to you was not in vain; we both know that.*

hose of us who *do* believe will enter His tranquil rest—not death.

Isaiah 57:1,2 . . . The godly man is removed from evil, he enters into peace. . . .

Hebrews 11:5 By faith Enoch was taken up by God before he was dead and wasn't found again. He obtained the witness that he was pleasing to God before he was taken up.

II Thessalonians 3:16 May the Lord of peace Himself continually grant you peace in every way.

Romans 15:33 The God of peace be with you. . . .

Romans 16:20 The God of peace will soon crush Satan under your feet.

II Corinthians 13:11 Siblings (in Christ) be happy, be fulfilled, be comforted, be of the same mind, live in peace; and the God of love and peace shall be with you.

Philippians 4:9 Practice the things you have seen and heard and learned from me, and the God of peace shall be with you.

I Thessalonians 5:23 May the God of peace Himself purify you entirely; and may your spirit and soul and body be preserved complete, and without guilt when our Lord Jesus Christ comes.

Hebrews 13:20 . . . The God of peace . . . through the blood of Jesus our Lord [validated] the everlasting will and testament between man and God. . . .

As opposed to those of whom He said, "As I swore in My wrath, they shall not enter My rest."

Psalm 95:11 "Therefore, I swore in My wrath, the truth is they shall not enter My rest."

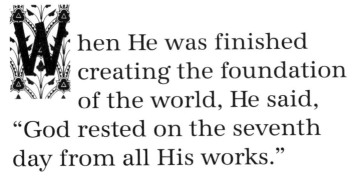

hen He was finished creating the foundation of the world, He said, "God rested on the seventh day from all His works."

Exodus 20:11 In six [epoch] days the Lord (YHWH) made the heavens and everything in them, and the earth and everything in it, and the sea and all that is in it, then rested on the seventh day. Therefore the Lord (YHWH) put his blessing on the seventh [epoch] day and made it a holy day of peace and rest.

Exodus 31:16,17 <u>The Lord instructing Moses what to tell all Israel</u> 'The sons of Israel shall observe the sabbath to celebrate the day of peace and rest throughout their generations as a perpetual agreement. It is a sign between Me and the descendants of Israel forever; because in six [epoch] days the Lord (YHWH) made heaven and earth, but on the seventh day He ceased from labor, and refreshed Himself.'

od also said, "They shall not enter My rest."

[This is a reference again to Psalm 95:11.]

 herefore, it follows that some shall enter God's tranquil rest—not death;

Revelation 3:1 "And to the angel of the church in Sardis write: 'He who has the seven Spirits of God, and the seven stars, says this: I know your deeds; I know your name and that you are alive, but yet you're dead.'"

[Compare to Hebrews 3:11, page 88.]

John 8:51,52 <u>Jesus speaking</u> "With absolute truth I tell you: anyone of you who keeps My Word shall never die."

Matthew 16:28 <u>Jesus speaking</u> "I tell you the absolute truth, there are some of those who are standing right here who shall not experience death until they see the Son of Man coming in His kingdom."

Yet those who formerly heard good news preached to them failed to enter the tranquil rest because they disobeyed God.

Revelation 6:11 Each of them was given a white robe and told that they should rest a little longer, for the number of their fellow servants who were to be killed as they they had been was not yet complete.

Matthew 11:29,30 <u>Jesus speaking</u> "Try on my yoke [bondage] yourself and learn from Me, for I am gentle and humble in heart, and you shall find *rest for your souls.*" [Note: A yoke represents bondage and servitude to the Master. Jesus was God's servant. We are supposed to be Jesus's bonded servants or bondaged servants.]

He again fixes a certain day for rest—"today". Since Joshua had obviously not given the sons of Israel a Sabbath day to rest,

God said through David, "*Today,* if you hear His voice, do not harden your hearts."

Psalm 95:8 Do not harden your hearts today if you hear His voice calling like (they did) at Meribah, like the time of Massah in the wilderness.

here remains, therefore, a Sabbath rest for God's people to observe.

Exodus 31:16,17 <u>The Lord instructing Moses what to tell all Israel</u> 'The sons of Israel shall observe the sabbath to celebrate the day of peace and rest throughout their generations as a perpetual agreement. It is a sign between Me and the descendants of Israel forever, because in six [epoch] days the Lord (YHWH) made heaven and earth, but on the seventh day He ceased from labor and refreshed Himself.'

he one who enters God's tranquil rest—not death—*is also the one* who rests from his work, as God did from His own.

Revelation 14:13 . . . A voice from heaven said, "Write: 'Blessed are the dead who die in the Lord from now on!'" "Yes," said the Spirit, "they may take a rest from their labors because their deeds follow after them."

et's not disobey resting on the Sabbath. We shouldn't fail God by repeating the disobedience of those (who were not faithful).

Revelation 21:7,8 "The one who overcomes shall inherit these things. I will be his God and he will be My son. As for the coward-hearted and non-believers and detestable murderers and immoral persons and those who practice witchcraft and worship false gods and all liars, their part will be in the burning lake with fire and brimstone, which [for them] is the second death."

Revelation 22:14,15 Those who cleanse themselves are blessed in that they will have the right to the tree of life and to enter the (holy) city [new Jerusalem]. Outside the city are the sodomizers and those who practice witchcraft and the immoral persons and murderers and those who worship false gods and everyone who loves and makes a practice of lying.

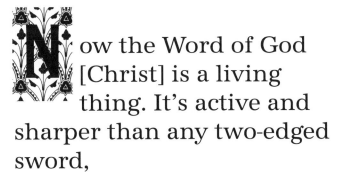

ow the Word of God [Christ] is a living thing. It's active and sharper than any two-edged sword,

---

I Peter 1:23 You have been born a second time, not of a perishable seed, but an imperishable seed, that is, through the living and abiding Word of God.

Jeremiah 23:29 "Is not My Word like fire?" declares the Lord (YHWH), "and like a hammer which shatters a rock?"

I Thessalonians 2:13 . . . The Word of God . . . accomplishes Its own work in those of you who believe.

Ephesians 6:17 Take the helmet [the knowledge] of salvation and the sword of the Spirit [that fights off evil], which is the Word of God.

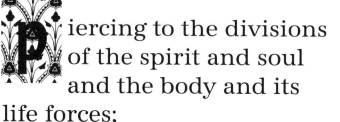

Piercing to the divisions of the spirit and soul and the body and its life forces;

Ephesians 1:17 <u>Paul prays</u> "May the God of our Lord Jesus Christ, the Father of glory, give you a spirit of wisdom and of revelation in the knowledge of Him."

ble to judge not only
the thoughts, but also
the intentions.

John 12:48 <u>Jesus speaking</u> "The one who rejects Me,
and doesn't receive My Words, has One Who judges
him; the Word I spoke is in fact what will judge him at
the last day."

Deuteronomy 18:19 "It shall happen that whoever
does not listen to My Words which the prophet shall
speak in My name, that one shall have to answer to
Me."

John 5:38,39 <u>Jesus speaking</u> "You do not have His
Word living in you, for you do not believe the One
Whom God sent. You search the scriptures because
you think that they will provide you with the secret to
everlasting life; and yet it is these very scriptures that
bear witness of Me, and you are still unwilling to come
to Me, so that you may have [the] life."

John 8:43,47 <u>Jesus speaking</u> "Do you know why you don't understand what I'm saying? It's because you cannot hear My Word. He who is of God hears the Words of God. You don't hear them because you are not of God."

Revelation 22:18,19 I solemnly declare to everyone who hears the words of the prophecy of this book: if anyone adds to these, God shall add to that one the plagues which are written about in this book; and if anyone takes away from the words of the book of this prophecy, God shall take away his portion in the tree of life and in the holy city, which are written about in this book.

 **A**ll things are seen by Christ, (the One Who is the reason we're here).

Psalm 33:13-15 The Lord looks from his dwelling place and sees all the families of man. He looks out on all the inhabitants of the earth, being the One Who forms the hearts of them all, and thus understands what makes them tick.

II Chronicles 16:9 The eyes of the Lord move here and there over all the earth, so that He may give strong support to the one whose heart is completely His.

Job 34:21,22 He looks at the ways of a man and sees all his steps. Though one tries to hide his sin in darkness or deep shadows, a man cannot hide from God.

 et's continue to confess
to our high priest,
Jesus, the Son of God.

Hebrews 3:1 Siblings in [Christ], you were tapped for God's own purposes. Think about Jesus—He was sent by God to teach and be our high priest.

Isaiah 53:12 Prophesying regarding the Messiah . . . He gave of Himself even to death, being numbered with the sinners. He Himself bore the guilt of many and *interceded for* the real sinners.

n fact, we do have a high priest Who can sympathize with our weaknesses because He has been tempted Himself, just like us,

Luke 4:1-13 Jesus, filled with the Holy Spirit, coming back from the Jordan, was led about by the Spirit in the wilderness for forty days while being tempted at the same time by the devil. He ate nothing during that time and was hungry once the forty days ended. The devil said to Jesus, "If You are indeed the Son of God, tell this stone to transform into bread." Jesus said, "In the scriptures it is written, 'Man shall not survive only on bread.'" Satan led Jesus up and showed Him all the kingdoms of the inhabited earth in a mere moment of time, saying to Him, "I will give You absolute ownership and control over this land with magnificence because it has been handed over to me and I can give it to whomever I want to. So if You worship me, I will give it to You." Jesus said to Satan, "In the scriptures it is written, 'You shall worship the Lord (YHWH) your God and serve no one but Him.'" Satan led Jesus to Jerusalem and set Him at the top most part of the temple, and said to Him, "If indeed You are the Son of God, throw Yourself down from the

temple since it's written in the scriptures, 'He will charge His angels with all concerning You to guard You', and also, 'they will hold You up with their hands, so that You won't even stub Your toe on a stone and stumble.'" Jesus answered saying, "It is said in the scripture, 'Don't test the Lord your God.'" So when the devil had tried every temptation, he left Jesus alone until a more opportune time.

Isaiah 53:10 <u>Prophesying about the Messiah</u> The Lord (YHWH) was pleased to crush Him, putting Him to great sorrow. If He put Himself up as a guilt offering, He will see His children.

nd still He is sinless.

Hebrews 7:26 It was fitting that we should have such a high priest Who is holy, innocent, pure in thought and deed, separated out from us sinners, and held up in glory above the heavens.

II Corinthians 5:21 God made (Christ), Who never sinned, to actually become sin on our behalf, so that in turn we might become the perfect goodness of God that was in Him.

I John 3:5 And you know that (Jesus Christ) appeared so that He would remove sin, and that there is no sin in Christ.

I Peter 2:22 Quoting Isaiah 53:9 ". . . (Christ) committed no sin, nor was any deceit found in His words."

Isaiah 53:9 His grave was assigned with practicing sinners, yet [He received one] with a rich man at His death, although He had committed no violence, nor was there any deceit in His words.

Let's go up with confidence to God's seat of forgiveness so that we can receive mercy and kindness to help us through the tough times.

Revelation 20:12 I saw the dead, the great, and the lowly standing before the throne, and books were opened, and another book was opened that is the book of life. Then the dead were judged from the things which were written in the books, corresponding to their deeds.

Revelation 22:3 There shall no longer be any curse, and the throne of God and of the Lamb shall be in it (the "holy city, new Jerusalem"), and His bond-servants shall serve Him.

Isaiah 25:8,9 He will put an end to death for all time. The Lord (YHWH) God will dry everyone's tears. The Jews' disgrace will be removed from all the earth because the Lord (YHWH) has said that He would do it. In that day people will say: "Look, this is our God Whom we have waited for, so He might save us. This is the Lord (YHWH) for Whom we have been waiting! Let's celebrate His salvation."

Revelation 7:17 "The Lamb, at the center of the throne, shall shepherd *them*, and guide them to the springs of the waters of life, and God shall wipe every tear away from their eyes."

Every high priest is appointed by God on behalf of other men and women so that they can offer gifts to God and sacrifices for human sins.

Hebrews 8:3 Now every high priest is appointed to offer both gifts and sacrifices, so he must have something to offer.

Exodus 24:4,5 Moses wrote down all the words of the Lord. Then he got up early in the morning and built an altar at the foot of the mountain. He built it with twelve pillars standing for the twelve tribes of Israel. He sent for the young men of Israel, and they offered burnt offerings and sacrificed young bulls as peace offerings to the Lord (YHWH).

Exodus 28:1 "Then take from the sons of Israel Aaron, your brother, and his sons; bring them into your confidence to minister as priest to Me—Aaron and Aaron's sons Nadab, Abihu, Eleazar and Ithamar."

Being human, the high priest can deal gently with those who are ignorant or misdirected, because the high priest himself is weak in so many things.

Galatians 6:1 Brothers, even if a man is caught in a sin, since you are spiritual, bring him back in a spirit of gentleness, watching out for your own self, so you won't be tempted, too.

Hebrews 7:28 The Law, you know, appoints as high priests men, who are naturally weak. But the Word of God's oath, which came after the Law, appoints His Son, made perfect forever.

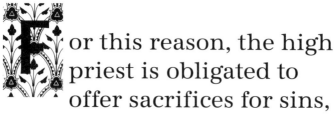 or this reason, the high priest is obligated to offer sacrifices for sins, for the people *and* for himself.

God's detailed instruction for sacrificial sin offerings

Leviticus 9:7 Moses said to Aaron, "Come to the altar and make your sin offering and your burnt offering so you make atonement for yourself and for the people; then make the offering for the people so that you make atonement for them, just as the Lord (YHWH) commanded."

Leviticus 16:1-34 The Lord (YHWH) spoke to Moses after Aaron's two sons had died approaching the presence of God. And the Lord said, "Tell your brother Aaron that he shall not enter at any time into the holy place inside the veil to stand before the mercy seat on the ark unless he wishes to die, because I am going to be in a cloud over the mercy seat. Aaron shall go into the holy place with this: a bull for a sin offering and a ram for a burnt offering. He shall put on the holy linen tunic over the linen underwear; he shall tie on a linen sash and wear a linen turban (for these are holy

garments). He shall bathe first and then put them on. And he shall get from the sons of Israel two male goats for a sin offering and one ram for a burnt offering. This bull, Aaron shall offer up as the sin offering for himself, so that he may request forgiveness and make amends (atone) for himself and the Levites. The two goats, he shall take and present them before the Lord (YHWH) in the entrance of the meeting tent. Aaron shall cast lots for the two goats, one lot for the Lord (YHWH) and the other for the scapegoat. The goat on which the lot for the Lord (YHWH) fell, Aaron shall offer as a sin offering. But the goat on which the the scapegoat's lot fell shall be presented live to the Lord to make atonement upon it, to send it into the wilderness as a scapegoat.

So Aaron shall offer the bull of the sin offering, requesting forgiveness for himself and the Levites, and slaughter it. First, he shall take a firepan of fiery coals from on top of the Lord's altar plus two handfuls of

finely ground sweet incense, and bring them both inside the veil. Then he shall put the incense into the fire before the Lord (YHWH) lest he die, so the cloud of incense covers the mercy seat on the ark of the testimony. Finally, with his finger he shall sprinkle some of the blood of the [sacrificed] bull on the mercy seat on the east side and seven times in front of the mercy seat.

Next he shall slaughter the goat that is the sin offering for the people, and bring *its* blood inside the veil, and do the same with its blood as he did the bull's, sprinkling it on the mercy seat and in front of the mercy seat. In this way, he shall make atonement for the holy place because of the impurities and sins of the sons of Israel and for the meeting tent as well, which is impure because their impurities are at its center. When he goes in the holy place to make atonement, the meeting tent shall be empty until after he's come out, so that he may ask forgiveness and

make amends for himself and for the Levites and for all the assembly of Israel. After that, he shall go out to the altar of the Lord (YHWH) and make atonement for it, and take a little each of the blood of the bull and the blood of the goat, and dab it on the horns of the altar on each side. Then he shall sprinkle some of the blood on the altar itself seven times to cleanse it and consecrate it from the impurities of the sons of Israel.

Once he's finished making amends to purify the holy place, the meeting tent, and the altar, then he shall offer the live goat. Aaron shall put both his hands on the head of the live goat and confess to Me all the imperfections and all the sins of the sons of Israel, [symbolically] laying [their guilt] on the head of the goat before handing it to the man waiting to take it to the wilderness. The goat bearing all their imperfections [and guilt] shall be released in the wilderness to a solitary place. Aaron shall come back into the meeting tent and take off the linen clothing

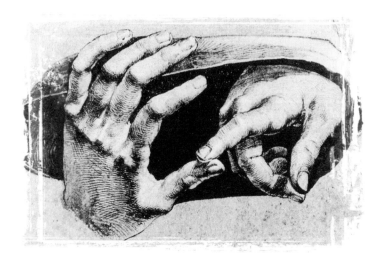

that he had put on when he went into the holy place and leave them there. He shall bathe with water in a holy place and put on his own clothes and come out and offer his burnt offering of the bull and the people's burnt offering of the one goat to request forgiveness and make amends for himself and for the people. Then he shall smoke the fat of the bull and the goat offerings on the altar and offer it up. The man who released the scapegoat shall wash what he was wearing and bathe with water, then come back into the camp. The [carcasses of] the bull and the goat of the sin offerings (whose blood was used to make atonement in the holy place) shall be taken outside the camp—their hides, and flesh, and refuse shall be burned in a fire. The person who burns them shall wash his clothes and bathe with water before coming into camp.

This shall be a permanent statute for you: on the tenth day of the seventh month, you shall humble your

souls and rest from all work, whether or not a native or foreigner who travels with you does the same. On that day atonement shall be made on your behalf so you'll be cleansed from all of your sins before the Lord (YHWH). It is a sabbath of serious rest for you, so you may humble your souls. This is a permanent statute. The priest, who is anointed and ordained to serve in his father's place [as his father before him did], shall put on the holy linen garments and make atonement for the holy sanctuary, the meeting tent, and the altar; he shall also make atonement for the [Levite] priests and for all the people gathered there. Now this is a permanent statute to make atonement for the sons of Israel for all their sins once every year." And Moses did exactly as the Lord commanded.

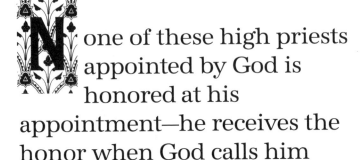

one of these high priests appointed by God is honored at his appointment—he receives the honor when God calls him (just as Aaron was called).

I Chronicles 23:13,14 The sons of Amram were Aaron and Moses. Aaron was selected especially to set him apart as most holy, both he and his sons forever, to burn incense before the Lord (YHWH), and to minister to Him, and to bless the Lord's name forever.

Numbers 18:6-8 <u>Lord speaking to Aaron</u> "Look, I Myself have selected your fellow Levites from the sons of Israel; they are a gift to you, dedicated to the Lord (YHWH), to perform service for the meeting tent. You (Aaron) and your sons need to tend to your priesthood including everything having to do with the altar and inside the veil; you are also to perform [the worship] service. I am giving you the priesthood as a gift of service, but the outsider who comes near shall be put to death." Speaking further to Aaron, the Lord said, "Now look, I Myself gave you charge of My offerings, and all of the holy gifts of the sons of Israel, I gave them to you as your portion, and to your sons as a perpetual allotment."

As opposed to . . .

II Chronicles 26:18 (The priests) opposed Uzziah the king and told him, "It is not for you, Uzziah, to burn incense to the Lord (YHWH) but only for the priests. . . . Get out of the sanctuary, for you have been unfaithful and will have no honor from the Lord God."

Likewise, Christ did not glorify Himself so as to become a high priest, but God said to Him, "You are my Son; today I have brought You forth in birth."

Jesus speaking

John 8:54 "If I give Myself glorify, it's meaningless; but My Father gives Me glory. My Father is the One you speak of when you say 'He is our God.'"

John 8:50 "I do not seek My own glory; there is One [the Father] Who seeks and judges."

John 12:23 "The hour has come for the Son of Man to be made glorious."

John 17:19-22 <u>Jesus praying to God</u> "For their sakes I purify Myself, that they also may be pure in Truth. I do not ask on behalf of these [that God gave Him out of the world—vs 6] alone, but also for those who put their faith in Me because of their words. I ask that they may all be united as if they were one. Just as You, Father, are in Me and I am in You, I ask that they also may be in Us, so that all inhabitants of the earth may believe that You did indeed send Me. The glory that You have given to Me, I have given to them so they may be one, just as We are One."

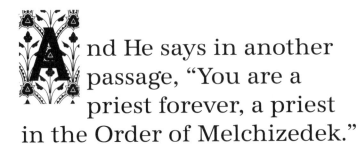

nd He says in another passage, "You are a priest forever, a priest in the Order of Melchizedek."

Psalm 110:4 The Lord (YHWH) swore [an oath] and is not going to change His mind. "You are a priest forever, a priest in the Order of Melchizedek."

Hebrews 7:13,14,16 The new high priest they were speaking about [Jesus] didn't belong to the Levite tribe [He didn't descend from Levi]. Instead, He belonged to a tribe from which no one had been an official at the altar. It's evident that our Lord was a descendent from Judah, and Moses never spoke anything regarding the tribe of Judah and the priesthood. . . . He [first Melchizedek, then Jesus Christ] didn't rise on the basis of the law of physical heritage, but rather rose on the power of an indestructible life.

Zechariah 6:13 <u>Prophesy about Christ, the Messiah</u> It is He (the man Whose name is "Branch") Who will bear the honor and build the temple of the Lord (YHWH), and He will rule from His throne. Thus He will be a priest on His throne [as well as a ruler], and the counsel of peace will be between them [the kingship and the priesthood].

<u>Introduction to Melchizedek</u>

Genesis 14:18-20 And Melchizedek, king of Salem, brought out bread and wine, for he was a priest of God Most High (El Elyon). And he blessed (Abraham) and said, "Blessed be Abram by God Most High, Who has delivered your enemies into your hand." And (Abraham) gave (Melchizedek) a tenth of all.

While Christ was in the flesh and blood and prayed and pleaded with God (Who was able to save Christ from death) in loud crying and tears,

Matthew 26:37-39 He took Peter with Him and the two sons of Zebedee [James and John] and started to grieve and get distressed. He said to them, "My soul is so sad and upset to the point of dying; stay here and keep watch with Me." Then He went a little ways away from them and fell on His face praying, "My Father, if it is possible, let this cup pass from Me; but do what You have wanted, Father, not what I want."

Mark 14:36 (Jesus) was saying, "Abba! Father! All things are possible for You; remove this cup from Me; yet not what I want, but what You have wanted."

Luke 22:42-44 (Jesus) said, "Father, if You are willing, remove this cup from Me; yet not My will, but Yours be done." Then an angel from heaven appeared to Him, strengthening Him. In agony, He prayed feverishly, and His sweat became like drops of blood, falling down to the ground.

e was heard by God, because of His godliness;

Matthew 27:46,50-54 About the ninth hour, Jesus cried out with a loud voice, saying, "Eli, Eli, Lama Sabachthani?", that is, "My God, My God, why have You forsaken Me?" . . . And Jesus cried out again in a loud voice and gave up His spirit. Then, the veil of the temple was torn in two from top to bottom, the earth shook, and the rocks were split. The tombs were opened, and many bodies of the saints who had fallen asleep were resurrected. Coming out of the tombs after His resurrection, they entered the holy city and appeared to many. When the centurion and his cohorts keeping guard over Jesus saw the earthquake and the things that were happening, they became quite afraid and said, "Truly this is the Son of God!"

ut although He was a Son, He suffered, and He learned obedience from these things that He suffered.

Acts 3:18 The things that God announced ahead of time through his prophets, that His anointed Messiah shall suffer, *He has fulfilled.*

Philippians 2:8 In His appearance as a man, He humbled Himself *by becoming obedient to God* to the point of death, death on a cross, yet.

John 10:17,18 <u>Jesus speaking</u> "The Father loves Me because I shall sacrifice My life so that I may live again. No one takes My life, but I put it to rest on My own initiative. I have authority to lay My life down and authority to take it up again. *My Father commanded Me to do so.*"

Romans 5:19 Just as through one man's (Adam's) disobedience many were made sinners, through the *obedience of the One (Christ)* many will be made righteous.

 e was perfected by God

II Corinthians 5:21 God made (Christ), Who never sinned, to actually become sin on our behalf, so that in turn we might become the perfect goodness of God that was in Him.

Hebrews 2:10 In bringing many sons to glory, it was fitting for Christ to perfect Himself as man's Saviour through suffering, as all things are made for Christ and made through Christ.

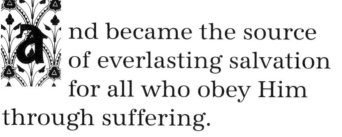

nd became the source of everlasting salvation for all who obey Him through suffering.

I Peter 1:14,15 As *obedient* children, don't maintain the former desires which you had while ignorant, but like the Holy One (Christ) Who called you, be holy yourselves in every thing you do.

I Peter 1:2 May forgiveness, mercy, and peace be yours in the fullest by the purifying work of the Spirit, according to God the Father's plan, so that you may *obey* Jesus Christ and therefore be sprinkled with His blood. [Note: Compare with the atonement, forgiveness and purification process described in Leviticus 16, pages 124-129.]

Acts 5:29 Peter and the apostles answered (the high priest and council), saying, "We must obey God rather than men."

Matthew 1:21 <u>Angel of the Lord speaking to Joseph, regarding Mary, in a dream</u> "She will have a Son and you shall call Him *Jesus*, for He is the One Who will save His people from their sins."

Isaiah 53:4-6 He bore our own griefs Himself, and our sadness weighed on Him; yet we thought He was afflicted of God. He was wounded for our sins. He was put down and crushed due to *our* own imperfection. It fell upon Him to *purify us* for our own well-being, and by His being thrashed, we are healed. He took on the discipline meant for us. We were the ones that went our own way, wandering off from God, but He took our guilt all on Himself.

Colossians 3:23-25 Whatever you do, do it from the heart like you're doing it for the Lord, rather than for men, knowing that you will receive the reward of inheritance from the Lord; it is Christ you serve. The person who does wrong things will receive the consequences of those acts without any partiality.

Psalm 103:19-22 The Lord (YHWH) has settled His throne in the heavens and He rules sovereignly over all. Bless the Lord, you His angels who are mighty in performing what He says, obeying the voice of His Word. All of you, His angels who serve Him, doing His will, bless the Lord. Bless the Lord, all of you created by Him, in all the lands of His kingdom. Oh soul of mine, bless the Lord!

He was, therefore, designated as a high priest according to the Order of Melchizedek [and in that role sacrificed *Himself* for our sins].

I Corinthians 15:3 I preached to you as a priority the words that I received myself–that is that Christ died for our sins according to Scriptures [and prophesy].

John 1:29 The next day (John, the Baptist) saw Jesus coming toward him, and said, "Look, there's the Lamb of God Who will abolish the sin of the world!"

Isaiah 53:7,10-12 He was oppressed and afflicted, and still He didn't say a word. Like a lamb led to slaughter and a sheep silent before its shearers, He didn't utter one word. The Lord (YHWH) was pleased to crush Him, putting Him to great sorrow. If He will put Himself up as a guilt offering, He will see His children. He will extend His life, His hand will perform the pleasure of the Lord (YHWH). As a result of the suffering of His soul, He will see all this and be satisfied. The Righteous One, My Servant, will justify the many with His knowledge [of God and man], as He will bear the guilt of man's sins. Therefore, I will allot

Him a portion with the great, and He will divide the takings with the mighty because He gave of Himself even to death, being numbered with the sinners. He Himself bore the guilt of many and interceded for the real sinners.

Romans 8:13 If you are living by human standards, you'll soon die; but if instead by the Spirit, then your sins will be put to death, and you will live.

Hebrews 9:15 Since Christ's death took place for the atonement of sins committed under the Law (the first Testament), then those who have been selected or tapped by God may receive the everlasting inheritance, which is God's promise. For this reason [His self-sacrifice], He is the mediator of a new contract between God and man [God's new Will and Testament].

In this regard, we have so much to say, and it's difficult to explain since you've become [so to speak . . .] hard-of-hearing.

By this time you ought to be teachers, but you still need someone to teach you from the start from the prophesies, and you still need milk, not solid food.

I Corinthians 3:1,2 Brothers, I could not speak to you as I would to spiritual men, but rather as to regular humans who are babies in Christ. I gave you milk to drink, not solid food, because you weren't yet able to digest it. Even now, you're not able.

 ach person who drinks milk only is a baby, not used to God's Word of what is right.

I Peter 2:1,2 Abandon meanness and lies, and pretenses [of piety] and jealousies and false statements defaming another's reputation. Long for the pure spiritual milk of the Word, like babies, so that by it you may grow up to receive salvation.

The mature can have solid food because through practice they have trained their senses to discern good and evil.

I Corinthians 14:20 Brothers, do not be children in your thinking (although definitely be babies in evil), but be mature in your thinking.

Ephesians 4:14,15 We should no longer be children, tossed here and there by waves and carried about by every wind of doctrine that comes along, by trickiness, or craftiness, or scheming lies. Truthfully, in love I say, we are to grow up in all aspects to be in Christ, Who is the head (of the body), yes, just like Christ.

So, God permitting, let's press on toward fuller development and perfection now that the foundation of teaching about the Messiah has been laid regarding:

[Verses are notated below to correspond to the referenced teachings numbered parenthetically (1)–(6) in Hebrews 6:1-3, pages 150-153.]

(1) John 14:23 Jesus said, "If anyone loves Me, he will keep My Word, so then My Father will love him, and We will come to him and stay with him."

Hebrews 9:14-17 Since Christ, through the everlasting Holy Spirit, offered Himself perfect to God, how much more will His blood cleanse your conscience from things you did leading to death under the Law, so you may serve the living God? Since Christ's death took place for the atonement of sins committed under the Law (the first covenant), then those who have been selected or tapped by God may receive the everlasting inheritance which is God's promise. For this reason [His self-sacrifice], He is the mediator of a new contract between God and man [God's Will and Testament]. Where there is a will, the one who makes it has to die

(1) being sorry and turning away from the disobedience that causes death; and (2) faith towards God;

[for the contractual will to be enforced]. It's, of course, never in force while the one who made it lives, since a Will and Testament is only valid when death occurs.

I John 1:6,7 If we say that we have close association with (Jesus) and we still walk on the dark side, then we're lying rather than practicing truth. If we walk in the light, as He Himself is in the light, we associate with each other, and the blood of Jesus, (God's) Son, cleanses us from all sin.

(1) and (2) *I John 5:1,2* Whoever *believes* that Jesus is the Messiah, that person is born of God; and whoever loves the Father loves the child conceived by the Father. When we love God and *observe* His commandments, then we know that we love the children of God.

I Peter 1:4-7 (God has caused us) to obtain an inheritance that cannot be cut short, is totally pure,

and (3) instructions about washings;

will not fade, and is reserved in heaven for you. You who are protected by the power of God through your faith for a salvation ready to be revealed in the last [epoch] day. Rejoice in this, for even though you may have been distressed for awhile by various tests, your *faith*, which is more precious than gold, may be proven this way. And, even though tested by fire, it may be found to result in praise and glory and honor when Jesus Christ is revealed.

(3) *Acts 22:16* <u>Paul recounting his revelation and calling and Ananias's last words to him (Ananias being a devout Jew)</u> "Now why do you delay? Get up off the ground and be *baptized, wash* away your sins, and call on God's (Righteous One's) name."

I Corinthians 6:11 And such were some of you [thieves, drunkards, swindlers, etc.], but you were *washed*, and purified, and atoned for in the name of the Lord Jesus Christ and in the Spirit of our God.

and (4) laying on of hands; and (5) the resurrection of the dead;

John 13:8,14,15 Peter said to (Christ), "You shall never wash my feet!", but Jesus answered, "If I don't *wash* you, you shall have no part of Me or My inheritance. . . . If I then, the Lord and Teacher, washed your feet, you ought also to wash each other's feet. [Follow My example and] do the same to each other as I have done for you."

(4) *Acts 19:6* Once Paul had *laid his hands* on them, the Holy Spirit filled them and they started to speak with tongues and started prophesying.

(5) *Revelation 1:5* Jesus Christ, Who loves us and released us from our sins with His blood, is the faithful witness, the firstborn of the dead, and the ruler of the kings of the earth.

and (6) eternal judgment.

John 6:39,40,44,54 "This is the will of God who sent Me, that I will lose nothing of all that He has given Me, but instead resurrect it on the last [epoch] day. The will of My Father is that everyone who looks upon the Son and believes in Him should live forever; and that I Myself will elevate that one [to glory] on the last [epoch] day. No one can come to Me unless My Father who sent Me draws that one to Me; that person I will resurrect on the last [epoch] day. He who partakes of My [sacrificed] body and My [poured out] blood will live forever, and I will resurrect him on the last day."

(6) *Jude 14,15* Enoch, in the seventh generation from Adam, prophesied, "Look, the Lord came with thousands and thousands of His holy ones to execute *judgment* on everyone, and to convict all the ungodly of all their ungodly acts done in an ungodly manner, and to convict the ungodly sinners who have spoken harsh things against Him."

II Peter 3:7 By His Word the present heavens and earth are being kept for the day of judgment and annihilation of ungodly men and reserved for fire.

Revelation 20:12 I saw the dead, the great, and the lowly standing before the throne; and books were opened, and another book was opened that is the book of life. Then the dead were *judged* from the things which were written in the books, corresponding to their deeds.

In the case of persons who fell away after they were enlightened and experienced a heavenly gift of the Holy Spirit,

Luke 8:13 <u>Jesus speaking</u> "Those on the rocky soil are those who, when they hear the word of God, are happy and excited, but they have no firm root; they believe for awhile, then when they are tempted, fall away."

Who have also experienced the good Word of God and have a sense of the powers of the coming age,

t's impossible for man to convert them again, since they crucify Christ a second time for themselves and shame Him openly.

Hebrews 10:26 If we go on willfully sinning after receiving knowledge of the truth, the sin offering no longer [pertains to] us.

II Peter 2:20-22 If, after they have overcome the sins of the world by knowing of the Lord and Saviour Jesus Christ, they become entangled in and are overtaken by them again, this last situation is worse than the first. It would have been better for them not to have known the Way of righteousness than to have turned away from the holy commandment delivered to them, once they knew the Way.

II John 9 Anyone who goes too far out on a limb and doesn't live by the teaching of Christ does not have God with him; on the other hand, the person who lives by the teaching has both the Father and the Son with him.

Hebrews 10:29 How much more severe do you think the punishment will be for the person who treats the Son of God like dirt and regards the blood of Jesus that validated His inheritance with God as impure and, further, has insulted the Holy Spirit of Grace?

Matthew 19:25,26 When the disciples heard this, they were shocked and said "If this is the case, then who can be saved?!" Looking at them Jesus said, "It seems impossible for man, but understand that with God all things are possible."

Let me give you this example: the field that continually soaks up rain and produces vegetation useful to those who work the field is blessed by God.

If the same earth would just produce thistle and thorns, it's totally worthless and, practically speaking, cursed, so it ends up being burned.

Dear ones loved by God, even though we are speaking rather negatively here,

I John 4:13 We know that we are living with God and that He's living with us because He has given us the Spirit.

II Peter 1:4 Through (Jesus Christ's divine power) He has granted His fabulous and highly prized promises so that you may participate in the divine nature, once having escaped the corrupt desires of the world.

II Peter 3:13 Based on His promise, we look forward to new heavens and a new earth filled with what is right and good.

we are convinced that better things will happen to you— things that go along with salvation.

Ephesians 2:4-7 God is rich in mercy; and, because of His great love for us, even though we were to die because of our sins, He made us alive through Christ. In other words, you've been saved by sheer kindness and mercy. Finally, He will raise us up with Christ and seat us with Christ in the heavenly places so that throughout the ages to come He might show us the richness of his kindness and mercy in the Christ, Jesus.

Ephesians 1:17 Paul prays "May the God of our Lord Jesus Christ, the Father of glory, give you a spirit of wisdom and of revelation in the knowledge of Him."

For God is not so unjust as to forget your work and the love you've shown Him by ministering to the saints as you have done, and still do.

I John 4:16-19,7 We have come to know and have believed the love which God has for us. God is love, and the one who lives in love lives in God, and God lives in him.

Since God lives in us and God is love, His love is perfected in us. By that, we should be confident in the period of judgment because we are in His love in the world.

Fear involves punishment, but there is no fear in love. The person who fears doesn't have perfect love because perfect love casts out fear.

Dear ones, let's love each other because love comes from God. We love because God loved us first. The love of all who love was born in God and they know God.

I John 2:1-3 My little children, I am writing these things to you so that you won't sin, and if anyone does, we have an Advocate with the Father, Jesus Christ, the perfect and good One. For He Himself is the request for forgiveness and the amends for our sins (atonement)—and not just for ours, but for all the inhabitants of the earth. We can say we know Christ if we are keeping His commandments.

I John 2:12 I am writing to you, little children because your sins are forgiven for the sake of the Lord Jesus.

It's our desire that each one of you is as diligent as ever so you'll be full of hope until the end.

I John 3:2,3 Dear ones, right now we are children of God, and it's not apparent what we shall be [in the new age]. We do know that, when Christ appears, we shall be like Him, because we shall see Him in His true state. Everyone who has this hope fixed on Christ purifies himself, just as Christ is pure.

Ephesians 1:18-23 I pray that the eyes of your heart may see and understand so that you may know what the hope of God's calling is, what the riches of the glory of His inheritance for the saints are, and what the exceeding greatness of his power is toward us who believe in Him. These go hand in hand with His mighty work in Christ, when He raised Christ from the dead and seated Him at His own right hand in the heavenly places, far above all rule, authority, power, and control, and persons in this age and in the age to come. He put all things in subjection under Christ's feet, giving Him as head over all things regarding the church; [He is the head], the church is the body, and everything is filled with Christ's completeness and power.

So that you won't be slow in this, just imitate the faithful and patient people who inherit God's promises.

II Peter 3:15,16 Look at the patience of our Lord as being critical to our salvation, just as our dear brother Paul does, who has written to you in wisdom given by God, speaking of these things in all of his letters. (Some of these things are hard to understand, so the untaught and unstable people distort them, like they do the rest of the scriptures, to their own detriment.)

Hebrews 13:7 Think about your leaders, who spoke God's word to you, and imitate their faith, remembering how they died for it.

James 1:2-4 [Dear] siblings in Christ, be happy when you are tested, since the very testing of your faith produces endurance. Let endurance work its own perfection in you, so that you may be mature and complete, with everything you need.

Hebrews 11:8-13 By faith Abraham, when called by God, obeyed by leaving home, with no clear destination, for a land that he was to receive as an inheritance from God. By faith he lived as an alien, a foreigner in the land promised to him, living in his tents with Isaac [his son] and Jacob [his grandson], fellow inheritors of the same promise. He was, of course, looking for the city Whose builder and architect is God. By faith, even Sarah herself received the ability to conceive a child, though she was way beyond the proper time of life, because she considered God, the One Who had given this promise, faithful. Out of that there was born, then, of one old man (close to death with regard to sexual matters) as many descendants as the stars of heaven in number and innumerable as the sand by the shore. All of these people died in faith, having confessed that they themselves were aliens and exiles on earth. Though they welcomed it from a distance, they died without receiving the promised inheritance.

Genesis 22:1,2,9-12 God tested Abraham, saying "Abraham!", who answered, "Here I am." God said, "Take your son, your only son, Isaac, whom you love and go right now to the country of Moriah and offer him up to Me as a burnt offering on one of the mountains of which I'll tell you." They came to the place that God had told him about, and Abraham built the altar and arranged the wood and bound his son Isaac and laid him on the altar over the wood. Then Abraham stretched out his hand with the knife to kill his son. But the angel of the Lord (YHWH) called to him from heaven, saying "Abraham, Abraham!", who answered, "Here I am." Then He said to Abraham, "Do not take the lad's life. Do nothing to him, for now I know that you have reverence for God since you have not withheld your only son from Me."

Revelation 13:10 If anyone is destined for captivity, to captivity he will go; if anyone kills with the sword, with the sword he must be killed. Here is [where] the perseverance and the faith of the holy ones [come in].

 ow, you know when God promised Abraham, He swore by Himself, since there was no one greater to swear by.

Genesis 22:16 The Lord (YHWH) declares "By Myself I have sworn, because you have done this [faithful] thing and not withheld your son, your only son. . . ."

nd He swore this: "I will surely bless you, and I will surely multiply you."

Genesis 22:17-18 "Indeed, I will bless you greatly and I will multiply your seed like the stars in heaven and like the sand on the shore; moreover, your seed shall possess the entrance to the land of His enemies. In your seed all the countries of the earth shall be blessed because you were obedient to My Voice."

 hus [Abraham], having patiently waited, obtained the promise.

Genesis 21:5 Abraham was one hundred years old when his son Isaac was born.

Galatians 3:16 The promises were given to Abraham and his seed. He does not say "and to seeds" (plural), referring to many, but rather "and to your seed", referring to one, meaning Christ.

As you know, to resolve disputes, men swear with an oath by someone greater than themselves.

Genesis 31:53 . . . So Jacob swore, out of respect for his father Isaac.

So God also swore an oath, wanting to show the inheritors of His promises the guaranteed permanency of His purpose.

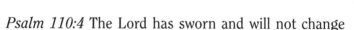

Psalm 110:4 The Lord has sworn and will not change His mind. . . .

With these two
permanent promises—

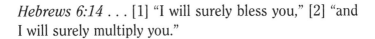

Hebrews 6:14 . . . [1] "I will surely bless you," [2] "and I will surely multiply you."

Genesis 15:5 (The Word of God came to Abraham, saying:) "Do you see the stars in heaven? Count them, if you can. Your descendants (seed) will be as numerous."

 t is impossible for God to lie—

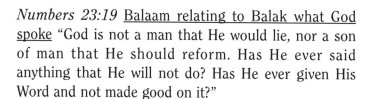

Numbers 23:19 <u>Balaam relating to Balak what God spoke</u> "God is not a man that He would lie, nor a son of man that He should reform. Has He ever said anything that He will not do? Has He ever given His Word and not made good on it?"

I Samuel 15:29 <u>The prophet Samuel speaking to King Saul</u> "The Glory of Israel will not lie or change His mind [like man], for He is not."

Ezekiel 24:14 "I, the Lord (YHWH), have spoken; it is coming and I shall act. I shall have no compassion, nor pity, nor shall I be sorry. I shall judge you according to your way of life and what you've done."

Titus 1:2 . . . God, Who cannot lie, promised eternal life a long, long time ago.

We who have fled [the status quo] for refuge [in Christ] can be strongly encouraged in holding fast to our hope.

Hebrews 3:6 Christ was faithful as God's Son ministering to God's people. As a body of believers, we belong to Christ if we have lasting belief, faith, and hope.

Hebrews 10:23 Let's get a good grip on our belief in our hope [of inheritance] [that is, resurrection and everlasting life] without wavering, because the Promiser is faithful.

This hope anchors our soul; it's both certain and constant and one which enters within the veil ("holy of holies").

Hebrews 9:1-3 The first Will and Testament even had regulations for worship of God and for the earthly dwelling place for God. There was an outer tabernacle prepared in which there were the lampstand and the table and the sacred bread—that's called "the holy place". There was another tabernacle behind the second veil called "holy of holies".

Leviticus 16:2 And the Lord said, "Tell your brother Aaron that he shall not enter at any time into the holy place *inside* the veil to stand before the mercy seat on the ark unless he wishes to die, because I am going to be in the cloud over the mercy seat."

Within the holy of holies, Jesus has entered as a front-man for us, as a permanent high priest, according to the Order of Melchizedek.

Hebrews 9:11,24 Alternatively, when Christ appeared as a high priest of a good inheritance, He entered through the greater and more perfect tabernacle that wasn't created by man. . . . Christ did not enter a holy place created by man, but entered into heaven itself to appear in front of God for us.

Hebrews 7:28 The Law, you know, appoints as high priests men, who are naturally weak. But the Word of God's oath, which came after the Law, appoints His Son, made perfect forever.

John 14:3 I will come back again and [you will come to Me and] I will receive you; so you'll be in the same place where I am.

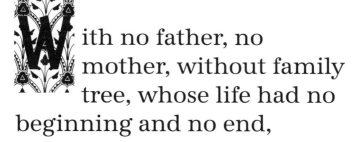

ith no father, no mother, without family tree, whose life had no beginning and no end,

Psalm 110:4 The Lord (YHWH) swore [an oath] and is not going to change His mind. "You are a priest forever, a priest in the Order of Melchizedek."

Hebrews 5:5,6 Likewise, Christ did not glorify Himself so as to become a high priest, but God said to Him, "You are My Son. Today I have brought you forth in birth." And He says in another passage, "You are a priest forever, a priest in the Order of Melchizedek."

Hebrews 7:6 Melchizedek['s] family heritage cannot be traced back to Abraham. . . .

Melchizedek was made like the Son of God and lives as a priest perpetually.

Melchizedek, King of Salem, was the priest of the Most High God who met Abraham, who was returning from a war with kings in which he had slaughtered them.

Melchizedek blessed Abraham, who set aside ten percent of all of his winnings.

Genesis 14:18-20 And Melchizedek, King of Salem, brought out bread and wine, for he was a priest of God Most High (El Elyon). And he blessed (Abraham) and said, "Blessed be Abram by God Most High, Who has delivered your enemies into your hand." And (Abraham) gave (Melchizedek) a tenth of all.

He gave them to Melchizedek, who was by the very translation of his name: "King of Righteousness", and secondly, "King of Salem", which means "King of Peace".

ook how great this man (Melchizedek) was to whom Abraham, the head of all the family of the Jews, gave ten percent of the choicest winnings from war.

Leviticus 27:30 All the *tithe of the land,* and of its seed, and of its fruit trees is the Lord's; it is holy to the Lord (YHWH).

[Definition of tithe: a tenth part of anything.]

And you know, the sons of Levi who were given (by God) the office of "priest" are commanded in the Law [of Moses]

Numbers 18:20,21 The Lord (YHWH) said to Aaron, "I am your portion and inheritance among the sons of Israel. You shall have neither inheritance nor ownership in any part of their land. As for the sons of Levi, look around you, I have given Israel's *entire tithe* for their inheritance in return for their service which they perform in the meeting tent."

to collect a tenth from their
Jewish brothers, all of them
being descendants of
Abraham.

But Melchizedek, whose family heritage cannot be traced back to Abraham, collected ten percent from Abraham,

[Compare Hebrews 7:1-3 on pages 179-183.]

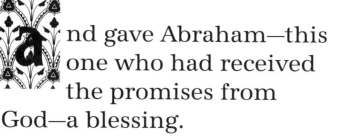**nd gave Abraham—this one who had received the promises from God—a blessing.**

Romans 4:13 The promise to Abraham or to his descendants that he would be heir of the world was not as a result of the Law, but as a result of the goodness of faith.

Now there can't be an argument—the greater being [in this case, Melchizedek] always blesses the lesser being [in this case, Abraham], [not vice versa].

In the case of [the Levitical priests], mortal men receive tithes;

[Compare Hebrews 7:5 on page 185.]

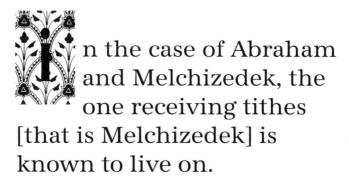

n the case of Abraham and Melchizedek, the one receiving tithes [that is Melchizedek] is known to live on.

Psalm 110:4 The Lord (YHWH) swore [an oath] and is not going to change His mind. "You are a priest forever, a priest in the Order of Melchizedek."

Hebrews 6:20 Within the Holy of Holies, Jesus has entered as a front-man for us, as a permanent high priest, according to the Order of Melchizedek.

One might say, through Abraham's [the father's] tithes to Melchizedek, even the Levite priests [Abraham's sons] paid tithes before Levi was ever born.

Numbers 18:26 "Moreover, you shall talk to the Levites and tell them I said, 'When you take the tithe from the sons of Israel which I have given you as your inheritance, you shall tithe a portion of it as an offering to the Lord, a tithe of the tithe.'"

hy would God see a need for another priest "to arise according to the Order of Melchizedek",

Hebrew 7:18 Then the first [order] was set aside . . . because it was weak and useless.

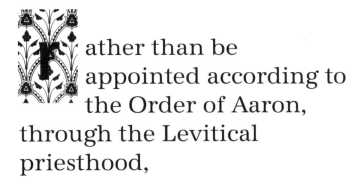

ather than be appointed according to the Order of Aaron, through the Levitical priesthood,

Exodus 28:1 "Then take from the sons of Israel Aaron, your brother, and his sons and bring them into your confidence to *minister as priest to Me*—Aaron and Aaron's sons Nadab, Abihu, Eleazar, and Ithamar."

God instructs Moses as to what to say to all Israel

Leviticus 1:7,9,11 'The sons of *Aaron, the priest*, shall build a fire on the altar and arrange wood over the fire. . . . Then *Aaron's sons, the priests*, shall smoke all of what is on the altar as a burnt offering, fire that has a soothing aroma to the Lord. . . . And he shall slay (the offering) before the Lord on the northward side of the altar, and Aaron's sons, the priests, shall sprinkle the blood of the offering all over the altar.'

Leviticus 3:1,2 'If this sacrifice is a peace offering (to the Lord), and (the priest is) going to take the animal, male or female, from the herd, then it must be perfect, with no defects. He shall lay his hand on the head of his offering and kill it in the entrance of the meeting tent; then *Aaron's sons, the priests*, shall sprinkle the blood of the offering all over the altar.'

Leviticus 4:31,35 'He shall remove all its fat, just like he did from the sacrifice of peace offerings, and the priest shall smoke it up over the altar to send up a soothing aroma to the Lord. In this way the *priest shall make amends* for him (the unintentional sinner) so that he may be forgiven.'

f indeed, one attains perfection through the Law, administered by the Levitical priesthood?

Hebrews 8:7-9 You know, if that first Will and Testament had been without a problem, then there would have been no need for a second. God, finding fault with it, said, "Understand, days are coming when I will put in effect a new Will and Testament with the House of Israel and the House of Judah, not like the one I made with their fathers on the day I led them by the hand out of Egypt—they didn't abide by the agreement and I didn't care for them anymore, says the Lord. . . ."

Hebrews 10:16,17 "This is the Will and Testament I will make with them at the close of the age, says the Lord: I will put my laws upon their heart and upon their mind I will write them." He then says, "And their sins and their lawless acts I will forget."

[One does *not*—vs 19]

Hebrews 10:1 Since the Law only foreshadows the good inheritance and is not the inheritance itself, it can never be the (legal) instrument to make perfect those who draw near to God by the same sacrifices year after year.

 he Law necessarily changed when the priesthood changed.

The new high priest they were speaking about [Jesus] didn't belong to the Levite tribe. [He didn't descend from Levi.]

Matthew 1:1-17 Matthew is the book of the family tree of Jesus Christ, son of David, son of Abraham. To Abraham was born Isaac, and to Isaac, Jacob; and to Jacob [whom God called "Israel"], Judah and his brothers along with Judah [these were 12 tribes of Israel, one of which was Levi from whose descendants the priests were appointed.] And to Judah . . . Perez . . . and to Perez was born Hezron; and to Hezron, Ram; and to Ram . . . Amminadab; and to Amminadab, Nahshon; and to Nahshon, Salmon; and to Salmon . . . Boaz . . . ; and to Boaz . . . Obed . . . ; and to Obed, Jesse; and to Jesse was born David the king. And to David . . . Solomon; . . . and to Solomon . . . Rehoboam; and to Rehoboam, Abijah; and to Abijah, Asa; and to Asa . . . Jehoshaphat; and to Jehoshaphat, Joram; and to Joram, Uzziah; and to Uzziah . . . Jotham; and to Jotham, Ahaz; and to Ahaz, Hezekiah; and to Hezekiah . . . Manasseh; and to Manasseh, Amon; and to Amon, Josiah; and to Josiah were born Jeconiah and his brothers, at the time of the deportation to Babylon.

Instead He belonged to a tribe from which no one had been an official at the altar.

After the deportation . . . to Jeconiah . . . Shealtiel; and to Shealtiel, Zerubbabel; and to Zerubbabel . . . Abiud; and to Abiud, Eliakim; and to Eliakim, Azor; and to Azor . . . Zadok; and to Zadok, Achim; and to Achim, Eliud; and to Eliud . . . Eleazar; and to Eleazar, Matthan; and to Matthan, Jacob; and to Jacob . . . Joseph, the husband of Mary, to whom was born Jesus, Who is called the Christ. (Fourteen generations each from Abraham to David, from David to the Babylonian deportation, and from the deportation to the time of Christ.)

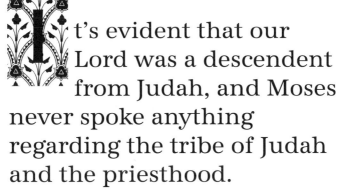 t's evident that our Lord was a descendent from Judah, and Moses never spoke anything regarding the tribe of Judah and the priesthood.

Micah 5:2 "But as for you, little Bethlehem Ephrathah, though you are too small to be counted among the clans of Judah, One will go out from you to be ruler for Me in Israel. His appearances are from long ago, since forever."

Isaiah 11:10,1-5 It will come about . . . that the [gentile] nations will resort to the *root* of Jesse. He will be there as a physical embodiment of God's message to the peoples, for His [tomb] will be glorious. [Note: Use of the term *root* rather than *branch*, possibly means the gentiles will resort to Christ *before* His root branches.]

A shoot will sprout from the stem of Jesse; it will branch from His roots and bear fruit. The Spirit of the Lord (YHWH) will rest on Him, so He will be full of the spirit of wisdom and understanding, the spirit of advice and might, the spirit of knowledge and respect for the Lord. He will take pleasure in pleasing the Lord.

He won't rely on what He sees and hears, but with perfect goodness He will rightly judge the poor and fairly decide for the desperate and suffering. He will [judge] the earth with the rod of His mouth, [the Word of God]; [His Spirit] will kill the wicked. Perfect goodness is His bare essential, faithfulness His support.

Revelation 5:5 . . . One of the elders spoke to me, "Don't cry; look, the Lion, the Root of David, from the tribe of Judah has overcome so that He may open the book and its seven seals."

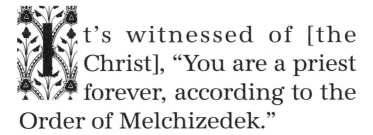

t's witnessed of [the Christ], "You are a priest forever, according to the Order of Melchizedek."

Psalm 110:1-4 <u>David prophesying about the Messiah</u>
The Lord (YHWH) says to my Lord: "Sit at My *right hand* until I make Your enemies a footstool for Your feet." The Lord (YHWH) will stretch forward Your strong scepter from Zion, saying, "Rule in the middle of Your enemies." Your people will volunteer freely in the day of Your power. In holy array, Your youths surface like the dew born of dawn. The Lord (YHWH) swore [an oath] and is not going to change His mind. "You are a priest forever, a priest in the Order of Melchizedek."

But still, if another priest is to arise like Melchizedek, who didn't rise on the basis of the law of physical heritage, but rather rose based on the

Hebrews 9:25-28 And He doesn't have to enter . . . continually, each year, as the high priest enters the holy place. Otherwise, He would have needed to suffer many times since the beginning of the world; but instead, only once He has been manifested [as human] to put away sin at the consummation of the world by the sacrifice of Himself. It's appointed for man to die once and afterwards face judgment. Likewise Christ, Who suffered once for the sins of many, shall appear a second time and not that time to bear sin, but to [judge] those who eagerly wait for Him for their salvation.

I Peter 1:23-25 You have been born a second time, not of a perishable seed, but an imperishable seed, that is, through the living and abiding Word of God. For "people are like grass, and all their beauty is like the flower of of the field. The grass withers, and the flower fades, but the Word of God lasts forever." Mark this, the Word that was preached to you.

power of an indestructible life,

Revelation 11:15-17 . . . There suddenly were loud voices in heaven: "The whole world has become the kingdom of our Lord, and of His Christ, and He will reign forever and ever." And the twenty-four elders, sitting on their thrones before God, fell on their faces and worshiped Him: "Thank you, O Lord God, Almighty Who is and always has been, You have taken Your great power and have begun to reign."

hen the first [order] was set aside because (1) it was weak and useless (and did not make anything perfect after all),

Romans 8:1-4 No longer is there death for those who belong to Christ Jesus because you have been set free from the law of sin and death by the law of the Spirit, which is life in the Christ, Jesus. The [Mosaic] Law could not save us from sins because we're weak. But God saved us anyway, sending His own Son in the likeness of sinful man as a sin offering. He put sin to death in the flesh, but the requirement of the Law is fulfilled in us who walk [in the way of goodness and truth and faith] in accord with the Spirit of God.

Acts 13:39 "Through (Christ), everyone of you who *believes* is freed from all things by which you were enslaved under the Law of Moses."

Galatians 3:21 Does the [Mosaic] Law conflict, then, with the promises of God? May it never be [said]! Perfection and goodness would indeed have been based on it if a law had been given that was able to grant everlasting life.

nd (2) a better hope came about and, through that hope, we come closer to God.

Galatians 3:22 The scripture, on the other hand, has boxed us all into sin so that the promise might be given to those who believe by faith in Jesus Christ.

I Corinthians 2:9 You know, it's written, "Things that (the) eye hasn't seen and (the) ear hasn't heard, and that are not even yet desired by man, these are the things that God has prepared for the ones who love Him."

I Corinthians 6:14 God not only raised the Lord (Jesus), but God will raise us, too, through His power.

I Corinthians 7:23 God bought and paid for you; [how dare you] become slaves of men [rather than servants of God].

Lamentation 3:57 You drew near when I prayed to You, and You said, "Don't be afraid!"

Psalm 145:18 The Lord stays close to all who pray to Him, to all who pray to Him truthfully.

Isaiah 41:8-10 You, Israel, are My servant Jacob, who I chose, descended from Abraham, My friend. I have taken you from all over the globe, and even from its remote corners, and said to you, "You are My Servant, I chose you instead of rejecting you. Don't be afraid because I am with you; don't look over your shoulder for Me, for I am your God. I'll strengthen you and certainly help you. Rest assured, I will hold you up with My pure and just right hand [i.e., Christ—Matthew 26:54]."

Isaiah 41:14 "Don't be afraid, sons of Jacob, men of Israel; I'll help you," the Lord (YHWH) states emphatically. "Your Saviour is the Holy One of Israel." [Note: Holy One of Israel is the Messiah/Christ.]

Psalm 24:3-6 Who will be allowed to come up to God's [Mountain of Zion]? Who will be permitted to stand in the holy place [in His tabernacle]? [The answer is this:] the one who is innocent in action and intent, who hasn't given his soul over to lies or sworn with clever mis-statements. This one shall be blessed with perfection and goodness from the God Who saved him. Such shall be the generation of those who seek (their Saviour), even Israel.

This (new priesthood) [unlike the Levitical priesthood] was established with God's oath— He swore, "The Lord has sworn

Numbers 23:19 Balaam relating to Balak what God spoke "God is not a man that He would lie, nor a son of man that He should reform. Has He ever said anything that He will not do? Has He ever given His Word and not made good on it?"

I Samuel 15:29 the prophet Samuel speaking to King Saul "The Glory of Israel will not lie or change His mind [like man], for He is not."

Romans 11:29 The gifts of God and the calling of God [in this context to the Jews] cannot be revoked.

and will not change His mind. You are a priest forever."

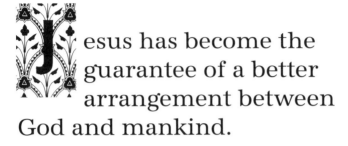

esus has become the guarantee of a better arrangement between God and mankind.

Hebrews 8:6 Jesus has obtained (from God) a more excellent ministry since He is also the mediator for a better Will and Testament, which has begun with better promises [of inheritance].

Jeremiah 31:31-34 "Watch now, the days are coming," announces the Lord, "when I will make a new Will and Testament [benefiting] the house of Israel and the house of Judah, not like the agreement I made with their ancestors when I took them out of Egypt. That agreement they broke, even though I cared for them as a *husband*. This is the Will and Testament that I will make for the house of Israel for later days," announces the Lord. "I will put My law inside them and write it on their heart. I will be their God, and they shall belong to me. They won't teach each other, saying, 'Know the Lord', because they'll all know Me, great and small," announces the Lord (YHWH), "because I'll forgive their impurity and forget their sin."

 here had to be a greater number of the former priests because they die off.

Jeremiah 33:17-22 The Lord says this: "David's line to the throne shall never be cut off, for Israel and the Levitical priests shall never have their line cut off in order to offer burnt offerings and burnt grain offerings and continual sacrifices." The Word of the Lord (YHWH) came to Jeremiah, saying, "Certainly you cannot break My will for the day and My will for the night that they fall at their appointed time. Neither can My will be broken for the Levitical priests, My ministers, nor for David, My servant–that he shall have a son to reign on his throne. The angels of heaven cannot be counted, the sand of the sea cannot be measured, and I will multiply the descendants of David, My servant, and the Levites who minister to Me, as those."

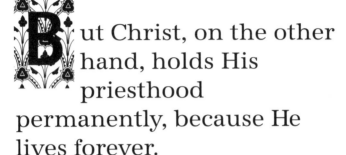

But Christ, on the other hand, holds His priesthood permanently, because He lives forever.

Hebrews 7:17 It's witnessed of [the Christ]: "You are a priest forever."

Psalm 110:4 The Lord (YHWH) swore [an oath] and is not going to change His mind: "You are a priest forever, a priest in the Order of Melchizedek."

Revelation 1:17,18 When I saw Him, I fell at His feet like a dead man. He laid His right hand on me and said, "Don't be afraid; I'm the first and the last and the Living One; I died, but now, see, I am alive forever, and I have the keys to death and hell."

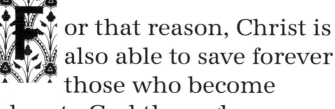

or that reason, Christ is also able to save forever those who become close to God through Himself,

Hebrews 10:12,14 But Christ, having offered just one sacrifice for all sins for all time, sat down at God's right. . . . By one offering He has perfected those who are set apart for purification.

 ince Christ always lives and can intercede on their behalf.

Romans 8:34 Who condemns (us) [to die]? Christ Jesus is the One Who died, yes, actually Who was raised from the dead, Who's at the right hand of God, interceding for us.

I John 2:1 My little children, I am writing all this to you so you won't sin. And if anyone does sin, our Advocate with the Father is Jesus Christ the perfect and good One.

Isaiah 53:12 Prophesying regarding the Messiah Because He gave of Himself even to death, being numbered with the sinners. He Himself bore the guilt of many and *interceded for* the real sinners.

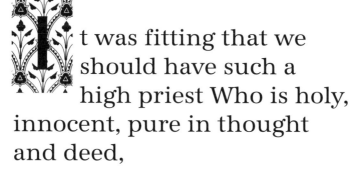

t was fitting that we should have such a high priest Who is holy, innocent, pure in thought and deed,

Hebrews 2:17 Christ of necessity had to be like His brothers in God so that He could be a merciful and faithful high priest, to make atonement, or reconciliation, with God for the sins of the people.

Hebrews 4:15 In fact, we do have a high priest Who can sympathize with our weaknesses because He has been tempted Himself, just like us, and still He is sinless.

II Corinthians 5:21 God made (Christ), Who never sinned, to actually become sin on our behalf, so that in turn we might become the perfect goodness of God that was in Him.

Isaiah 53:9 His grave was assigned with practicing sinners, yet [He received one] with a rich man at His death, although He had committed no violence, nor was there any deceit in His words.

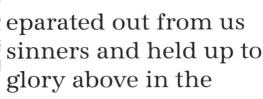

eparated out from us
sinners and held up to
glory above in the
heavens.

Revelation 5:6-10 I saw between the throne (in the middle of the four living creatures and the elders) a Lamb standing, as if slain, that had seven horns and seven eyes, which are the seven Spirits of God, sent out to all the earth. And [the Lamb] came and He took (the book) out of the right hand of the One who sat on the throne. When [the Lamb] had taken the book, the four living creatures and the twenty-four elders prostrated themselves before the Lamb, each having a harp and golden bowls of incense, that are prayers of the saints. They sang a new song: "You are worthy to take the book and break its seals, because You were killed. And with Your blood, You purchased for God men from every family and every language and every race and every nation. You have made them a kingdom and priests to our God, and they will exercise sovereign power over the earth."

A high priest Who also doesn't need to offer up sacrifices for His own sins and for the sins of the people on a daily basis, because He did it once and

Revelation 5:12-13 "The Lamb that was killed is worthy to receive power and riches and wisdom and might, honor, glory, and blessings." And I heard every created thing in heaven and on earth, all things under the earth and in the sea, saying, "May God, Who sits on the throne, and the Lamb have all blessing and honor and glory and control forever and ever."

Ephesians 5:2 The same way Christ loved you and gave His life for [you] as a sacrificial and fragrant offering to God, so you should walk in a like, loving manner.

John 1:29 The next day (John, the Baptist) saw Jesus coming toward him and said, "Look, there's the Lamb of God Who will abolish the sin of the world!"

for all time when He offered up Himself [as the Lamb].

I Peter 1:18,19 You know that you were redeemed with precious blood—the blood of Christ—as an unblemished and spotless lamb, not with silver or gold, perishable trinkets from the meaningless way of life passed down by your ancestors.

he Law, you know, appoints as high priests men, who are naturally weak.

Hebrews 5:2 Being human, the high priest can deal gently with those who are ignorant or misdirected, because the high priest himself is weak in so many things.

But the Word of God's oath, which came after the Law, appoints His Son, made perfect forever.

Psalm 110:4 The Lord (YHWH) swore [an oath] and is not going to change His mind: "You are a priest forever, a priest in the Order of Melchizedek."

Revelation 11:15 . . . There suddenly were loud voices in heaven: "The whole world has become the kingdom of our Lord and of His Christ; and He will reign forever and ever."

Revelation 4:8-11 The four living creatures, each one with six wings, are full of eyes inside and out; and day and night they never rest, but say, "Holy, holy, holy, the Lord God the Almighty, Who was, Who is, and Who is to come." When the living creatures give glory and honor and thanks to God, Who sits on the throne (the One Who lives forever and ever), the twenty-four elders will fall down before Him and worship Him. They will throw their crowns in front of the throne and say: "Worthy are You, our Lord and our God, to receive glory and honor and power as You created all things; because of Your will they existed and were created."

The main point of this discussion is this: we have as our high priest One that sits at the right hand of the throne of the Majestic King in Heaven [God];

Revelation 3:14,21 To the angel of the church in Laodicea write: "The Amen, the faithful and true Witness of God, the origin of the creation of God, says this: 'I will grant to the one who overcomes the right to sit down with Me on My throne, since I also overcame and sat down with My Father on His throne.'"

John 14:19,20 <u>Jesus speaking</u> "After a little while, the world will not see My face, but you will see Me; because I live, you shall live also [and overcome death]. Then you will know that I am in My Father, and you are in Me, and I in you."

Hebrews 10:12 But Christ, having offered just one sacrifice for all sins for all time, sat down at God's right.

high priest Who is a minister in the sacred temple and in the true, the real house of God, which the Lord set up—not man.

Revelation 11:19 The temple of God that is in heaven was open, and there in His temple appeared the ark of His covenant accompanied by [crashes of] lightning and peals of thunder, an earthquake, and a huge hailstorm.

Hebrews 9:11,23,24 Therefore it was necessary for our earthly copies of heavenly things to be cleansed with these (types of death and sacrifices). But the heavenly things themselves (are cleansed) with better sacrifices than these. . . . Alternatively, when Christ appeared as a high priest of a good inheritance, He entered through the greater and more perfect tabernacle that wasn't created by man. . . . Christ did not enter a holy place created by man, but entered to heaven itself to appear in front of God for us.

Revelation 1:5,6 Jesus Christ, Who loves us and released us from our sins with His blood, is the faithful witness, the firstborn of the dead, and the ruler of the kings of the earth. We are His kingdom and priests to God, His Father. . . . May Christ be glorious and dominant forever and ever. Amen.

Matthew 27:50,51 . . . Jesus cried out again in a loud voice and gave up His spirit. Then, the veil of the temple was torn in two from top to bottom, and the earth shook, and the rocks were split.

Mark 15:37,38 Jesus emitted a loud cry and died. The temple veil was torn into two pieces from top to bottom.

Luke 23:45,46 The sun was failing, and the veil of the temple was torn in half. Jesus cried out loudly, "Father I commit My Spirit into Your hands." At that moment, He breathed His last.

Exodus 26:33-34 "You shall hang the veil up with the clasps and bring the ark of the Testament in there behind the veil, and the veil shall serve as a divider between the holy place and the holy of holies. You shall put the mercy seat on the ark of the Testament inside the Holy of Holies [behind the veil]."

 ow every high priest is appointed to offer both gifts and sacrifices, so he must have something to offer.

God speaking to Moses

Leviticus 22:2 "Tell Aaron and his sons to be careful with the holy gifts from the sons of Israel that were dedicated to Me. They must not profane My holy name, for I am the Lord (YHWH)."

Leviticus 2:1 "When anyone presents a grain offering to the Lord (YHWH), this offering shall be fine flour with oil poured on it and frankincense put on it."

Leviticus 3:1 'If this sacrifice is a peace offering (to the Lord), and (the priest is) going to take the animal, male or female, from the herd, then it must be perfect, with no defects.'

Leviticus 7:1-3 "This is the law of the guilt offering, and it is most holy: In the same place as they kill the burnt offering they are to kill the guilt offering, and (the high priest) shall sprinkle its blood around the altar. Then he shall offer all its fat—the fat tail and the fat covering the guts."

ccording to the Law, Christ would not be a priest at all here on earth, since the Law already defines the Levites to act as priests and offer gifts.

Numbers 18:6-8 <u>Lord speaking to Aaron</u> "Look, I Myself have selected your fellow Levites from the sons of Israel; they are a gift to you, dedicated to the Lord (YHWH), to perform service for the meeting tent. You (Aaron) and your sons need to tend to your priesthood including everything having to do with the altar and inside the veil; you are also to perform [the worship] service. I am giving you the priesthood as a gift of service, but the outsider who comes near shall be put to death." Speaking further to Aaron, the Lord said, "Now look, I Myself gave you charge of My offerings, and all of the holy gifts of the sons of Israel, I gave them to you as your portion, and to your sons as a perpetual allotment."

Nehemiah 12:23 The sons of Levi that were fathers over households were registered in the Book of the Chronicles up until Johanan the son of Eliashib.

ut they only symbolize and foreshadow the real heavenly things. Moses was even warned by God when he was ready to erect the tabernacle:

Hebrews 9:23 Therefore it was necessary for our earthly copies of heavenly things to be cleansed with these (types of death and sacrifices). But the heavenly things themselves (are cleansed) with better sacrifices than these.

Colossians 2:16,17 Don't let anyone judge you with regard to what you eat or drink or as to a festival celebration or a new moon celebration or a Sabbath day. These things merely foreshadow what's coming; the substantial matters belong to Christ.

Hebrews 10:1 Since the Law only foreshadows the good inheritance and is not the inheritance itself, it can never be the (legal) instrument to make perfect those who draw near to God by the same sacrifices year after year.

 e sure that you make all things by the pattern I showed you on the mountain."

—Exodus 25:40

<u>As opposed to the real heavenly thing</u>

Revelation 11:19 The temple of God that is in heaven was open, and there in His temple appeared the ark of His covenant. . . .

Jesus has obtained (from God) a more excellent ministry, since He is also the mediator for a better Will and Testament,

I Corinthians 8:6 For us there is only one God, Who we call "Father", and everything came *from* Him, and we exist for God. Also (there is only) one Lord Jesus Christ, and everything came *through* Him, and we exist *through* Christ.

I Corinthians 11:25 He took the cup . . . after they had finished supper and said, "This cup creates God's new Will and Testament, [validated with] My blood for mankind; whenever you drink it, do so in My memory."

II Corinthians 3:6 (God) also made us adequate as servants of a new agreement, not of the letter (of the Law), but of the Spirit, for the letter (of the Law) [means certain death], but the Spirit gives life.

Hebrews 9:16-20 Where there is a will, the one who makes it has to die [for the contractual will to be enforced]. It's of course never in force while the one who made it lives, since a Will and Testament is only

valid when death occurs. That's why even the first Will and Testament was not put into effect without death. Moses first told all the commandments to the people. Then, according to what the Law said, he took the blood of the calves and goats with water and red wool and hyssop and sprinkled both the book (in which he had written all of God's words to him) and the people, saying: "This is the blood of the Will and Testament by which God commanded you."

Jeremiah 31:31 "Watch now, the days are coming," announces the Lord, "when I will make a new Will and Testament [benefiting] the house of Israel and the house of Judah."

Ephesians 2:8 By God's mercy you have been saved because of your faith, but you did not save yourself—(your salvation) is the gift of God.

Luke 22:20 Then He took the cup after they had eaten, and said, "This cup represents My blood poured out for you that creates God's new will for mankind."

I Timothy 2:5 There is one God, also one mediator between God and mankind, the man Christ Jesus.

Galatians 3:16-25 The promises were spoken to Abraham and to his seed. He doesn't say, "And to seeds," [plural] referring to many, but to your seed, just to one, that is, Christ. What I am saying is this: the Law, which came four hundred and thirty years later [through Moses], didn't invalidate God's Will and Testament, so as to void the promise [of inheritance]. Look at it this way, if inheritance is based on law, then it's not based on a promise; but we know God granted [the inheritance] to Abraham through promise. Why is the Law necessary then? It was added because of sins against God having been ordained through angels, through an intermediary, until the "seed" to Whom the

promise [of inheritance] has been made should come.
Does the [Mosaic] Law conflict, then, with the
promises of God? May it never be [said]! Perfection and
goodness would indeed have been based on it if a law
had been given that was able to grant everlasting life.
The scripture, on the other hand, has boxed us all into
sin so that the promise might be given to those who
believe by faith in Jesus Christ. [In other words] before
faith came into the picture, we were actually under
custody of the Law, locked away from the very faith
that was to be revealed later. So [we could say that] the
Law has become our tutor to guide us to Christ and to
justify our faith. And now that faith has come, we are
no longer under the tutor.

Galatians 3:26,29 All you are sons of God through
your faith in Christ Jesus. If you belong to Christ, then
you are Abraham's children and heirs of the promise [of
inheritance].

II Corinthians 3:6 (God) also made us adequate as servants of a new agreement, not of the letter (of the Law), but of the Spirit, for the letter (of the Law) [means certain death], but the Spirit gives life.

 hich has begun with better promises [of inheritance].

II Corinthians 3:9-11 Indeed, if the ministry of condemnation has glory, then the ministry of godly purity and goodness is full of glory. The fading glory (of the ministry of death) is surpassed by the lasting glory (of the ministry of the Holy Spirit).

Philippians 3:20,21 We are citizens of heaven, whereby we also eagerly wait for our Saviour, the Lord Jesus Christ. He will transform our humble bodies to conform to His glory by exerting His power to subject all things to Himself.

Colossians 1:19,20 It was the Father's desire for all the fullness [of the deity] to dwell in (Christ) and to reconcile all things to Himself through (Christ), having made peace [or reconciliation] through the blood of His cross. Through (Christ), I repeat, whether things on earth or in the heavens, [they were all reconciled to the Father].

I Thessalonians 4:14,15 Just as we believe that Jesus died and rose again, God will also raise those who have fallen asleep in Jesus and will bring them with Him. The Word of the Lord testifies that those who have fallen asleep shall precede those of us who are (still) alive at the coming of the Lord.

II Thessalonians 2:13,14 We should always thank God for you, brethren loved by the Lord, because God chose to save you from the start, through purification by the Spirit and through [your] faith in the truth. For this reason He called you through our true accounts (or gospel), so that you may receive the glory of our Lord Jesus Christ.

ou know, if that first Will and Testament had been without a problem, then there would have been no need for a second.

Hebrews 7:11 Why would God see a need for another priest "to arise according to the Order of Melchizedek", rather than be appointed according to the Order of Aaron, through Levitical priesthood, if indeed one attains perfection through the Law? . . .

od, finding fault with it, said, "Understand, days are coming when I will put in effect a new Will and Testament with the House of Israel and the House of Judah,

Jeremiah 31:31 "Watch now, the days are coming," announces the Lord, "when I will make a new Will and Testament [benefiting] the house of Israel and the house of Judah."

ot like the one I made with their fathers on the day I led them by the hand out of Egypt—

Jeremiah 31:32 "... [It will not be] like the agreement I made with their ancestors when I took them out of Egypt. ..."

 hey didn't abide by the agreement and I didn't care for them anymore, says the Lord.

Jeremiah 31:32 ". . . That agreement they broke, even though I cared for them as a *husband.*"

Isaiah 59:15,16 There's no truth anywhere, and the one who isn't evil becomes prey to those who are. The Lord was extremely upset that there was no justice, and He saw and was astounded that there was no man who could intervene in this. So His own [right] arm brought salvation to Him and His own perfection and goodness lifted Him up.

This is the will I will make for the House of Israel at the end of the age, says the Lord. I will put my Law in their [thoughts], I will etch it onto their hearts

Jeremiah 31:33 "This is the Will and Testament that I will make for the house of Israel for later days," announces the Lord. "I will put My law inside them and write it on their heart. I will be their God, and they shall belong to Me."

Isaiah 59:20,21 "One who will recover My people with a price will come to Zion, to those in Israel who turn away from sin. As for My part," says the Lord (YHWH), "neither My Spirit that is on you, nor My Words that I have put in your mouth shall leave you, nor leave the mouths of your children, nor their children, forever more."

[where they can feel it], and I will be their God, and they shall be My people.

There will be no need for anyone to teach his fellow countryman or his brothers, saying 'Know the Lord',

---

Jeremiah 31:34 "They won't teach each other, saying, 'Know the Lord', because they'll all know Me, great and small," announces the Lord (YHWH), "because I'll forgive their impurity and forget their sin."

Especially the nation of Israel

Jeremiah 24:7 The Word came to (Jeremiah): "Thus says the Lord God (YHWH) of Israel, 'They will know Me in their heart, as I am the Lord (YHWH). They'll be My people, and I'll be their God [when] they come back to Me wholeheartedly.'"

 or they will all know Me—from the least to the greatest.

Isaiah 11:9,10 In all My holy nation, nothing will hurt or destroy because the entire earth will be full of the knowledge of the Lord (YHWH)—as full as the seas. It will come about . . . that the [gentile] nations will resort to the *root* of Jesse. He will be there as a physical embodiment of God's message to the peoples, for His [tomb] will be glorious. [Note: Use of the term *root* rather than *branch*, possibly means the gentiles will resort to Christ *before* His root branches.]

For I will be merciful toward their impure thoughts and deeds and I will write off their sins and never recall them."

Jeremiah 31:34 ". . . I'll forgive their impurity and forget their sin."

Especially the nation of Israel

Jeremiah 50:20 "In that [epoch]," the Lord proclaims, "everyone will look for Israel's transgressions and Judah's sins, but they won't find any because I shall [have] pardoned those whom I have left as a portion of the great nation."

Isaiah 43:25 "I am the very same One Who wipes out your sins—not for your sake, but for Mine. I mean, I won't even remember your sins."

Micah 7:18-20 What other being exists who forgives sin and overlooks the rebellion of those saved out of his people like You do, God? God doesn't stay angry forever because constant love makes Him happy. Once again, He'll take compassion on us and stamp out our

sins, burying them at sea. You, God, will give Israel faith and to all Abraham's descendants, constant love. That's what You swore to our ancestors long ago.

Isaiah 55:7,8 Forsake your wicked life and bad, impure thoughts; return to the Lord (YHWH), our God. He'll take compassion on you and pardon everything. For the Lord (YHWH) says, "I think differently than you do. And so I act differently than you [might expect]."

II Corinthians 5:18,19 All this is from God, Who gave us the ministry of His peace through the Christ: that God was in Christ making peace with the inhabitants of the earth, overlooking their sins against Him. And we are committed to God to spread the Word of His peace with mankind.

hen God said, "a new will", He made the first one obsolete. And whatever is old or obsolete is practically gone already.

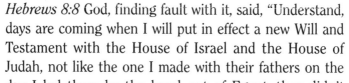

Hebrews 8:8 God, finding fault with it, said, "Understand, days are coming when I will put in effect a new Will and Testament with the House of Israel and the House of Judah, not like the one I made with their fathers on the day I led them by the hand out of Egypt—they didn't abide by the agreement, and I didn't care for them anymore. . . ."

Hebrews 7:22 Jesus has become the guarantee of a better arrangement between God and mankind.

II Corinthians 5:17 If any man belongs to Christ, then he [shall be] a new creation because what existed before [will be] gone, being replaced with new things.

The first Will and Testament even had regulations for worship of God and for the earthly dwelling place for God.

Exodus 26:30-33 "You shall build the temple just like the plan I showed you in the mountains. You shall have a veil made by very skilled workman, with cherubim angels and fine twisted linen material of blue, purple, and scarlet red. Hang it up on four pillars of acacia wood paneled in gold, with the hooks also being gold over four silver bases. You shall hang the veil up with the clasps and bring the ark of the Testament in there behind the veil, and the veil shall serve as a divider between the holy place and the Holy of Holies."

Exodus 25:40 "Be sure, now, you make it from the pattern I showed you in the mountains."

Exodus 25:9 "Construct (the sanctuary for Me) like what I am going to show you, just like you used (My) pattern for the temple and (My) pattern for all the temple furniture."

There was an outer tabernacle prepared in which there were the lampstand and the table and the sacred bread—that's called "the holy place".

Exodus 40:22-25 (Moses) put the table outside the veil in the north side of the tabernacle in the meeting tent. He set the bread on it in the orderly fashion that God had commanded him to do. The lampstand he placed on the south side opposite the table and he lit the lamps in front of God, as God had commanded him.

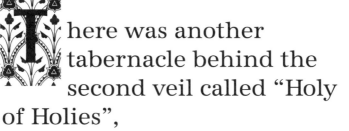 here was another tabernacle behind the second veil called "Holy of Holies",

Exodus 26:31,33 "You shall have a veil made. . . . Bring the ark of the Testament in there behind the veil, and the veil shall serve as a divider between the holy place and the Holy of Holies."

aving a golden altar of incense and the completely golden ark of the Testament,

Exodus 25:10,11 "They shall construct from acacia wood an ark that's 45" long and 27" wide and 27" high and lay gold over it, both inside and out, with a gold molding surrounding the ark."

Exodus 40:5 "Set the gold altar of incense in front of the ark of the Testament and (then) set up the [first] veil over the entrance to the tabernacle."

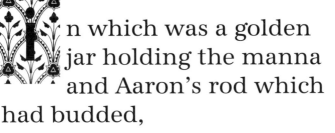

n which was a golden jar holding the manna and Aaron's rod which had budded,

Exodus 16:32-35 Moses said, "The Lord commanded this: 'Let a portion of the bread I fed you in the wilderness coming out of Egypt be stored so that your descendants may see it.'" So Moses told Aaron, "Put a portion of the manna in a jar and place it in front of the Lord (YHWH) for your descendants [to see]." [This was] the manna [that] the descendants of Israel ate for forty years until they came to the uninhabited border of Canaan.

Numbers 16:3-5 and 17:1-3,5,8,10,11 (Two hundred and fifty leaders) confronted Moses and Aaron, saying, "Why do you elevate yourselves above the rest of us; you've overstepped [your calling], because all of us are holy and the Lord is with *us*, too." Moses immediately fell on his face, then spoke to Korah and his gang: "Tomorrow morning the Lord will reveal who is His holy one and will bring that one close to Himself." The Lord said to Moses, then, "Speak to the descendants of Israel and ask them to give you a (wooden) rod from

each family tribe, in other words, twelve rods total.
Then write each name on that tribe's rod. Now the rod
of the (holy) man I choose will sprout. That ought to
quiet the grumblings of these men against you.". . .
The next day when Moses went into the meeting tent,
Aaron's rod, representing the family of Levi, had
sprouted buds, with blossoms and ripe almonds[!] The
Lord told Moses, "Put Aaron's rod in front of the
Testament so it will serve as a reminder to these rebels
that they shouldn't grumble against Me if they want to
live." Moses did just exactly as God commanded him.

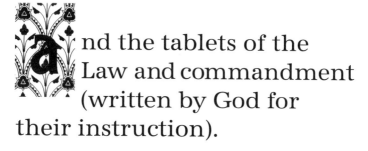

nd the tablets of the Law and commandment (written by God for their instruction).

Exodus 25:16,21 "I'll give you the Testament to put inside the ark. Put the mercy seat above the top of the ark and put the Testament that I will give you inside the ark."

Exodus 24:12 The Lord told Moses, "Come up the mountain and stay put. I'll give you the stone tablets with the Law and [ten] commandment[s] that I wrote for (Israel's) instruction."

And above (the ark of the Testament) there were the cherubim (angels) of glory over the mercy seat— but we can't speak in any more detail about this now.

Exodus 25:17-20 "Make a mercy seat out of pure gold that's 45" long and 27" wide and make two cherubim of hammered gold for each end of the mercy seat. Be sure to make the two cherubim as one piece, with the mercy seat attached at the two ends. The cherubim should have upward-spreading wings, facing each other, but with faces turned toward the mercy seat, covering the mercy seat with their wings."

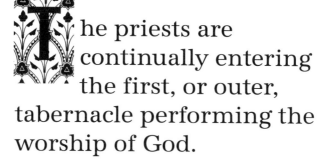

he priests are continually entering the first, or outer, tabernacle performing the worship of God.

Numbers 28:23 Tell the men of Israel, "You need to take care to present My offerings . . . at their appointed time. . . . You shall offer two perfect male lambs as a continual burnt offering every day."

Numbers 18:7 "You (Aaron) and your sons need to tend to your priesthood as pertaining to everything having to do with the altar and inside the veil; you are also to perform [the worship] service."

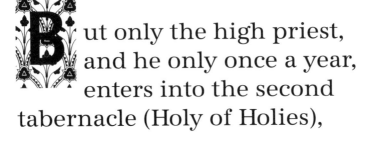

But only the high priest, and he only once a year, enters into the second tabernacle (Holy of Holies),

Exodus 30:30 "Anoint Aaron and his sons to set them aside for the Lord so they can minister to Me as priests."

Leviticus 16:2,34 And the Lord said, "Tell your brother Aaron that he shall not enter at any time into the holy place inside the veil to stand before the mercy seat on the ark unless he wishes to die, because I am going to be in a cloud over the mercy seat. Now this is a permanent statute to make atonement for the sons of Israel for all their sins once every year." . . .

lways taking blood to offer God for his atonement of sins and the sins of the people committed out of ignorance.

Leviticus 16:14 "Finally, with his finger he shall sprinkle some of the blood of the [sacrificed] bull on the mercy seat on the east side and seven times in front of the mercy seat."

Leviticus 16:17 ". . . [He shall do this] so that he may ask forgiveness and make amends for himself and for the Levites and for all the assembly of Israel."

he Holy Spirit is using this tabernacle structure to signify that the way to the holy place is not revealed as long as the first tabernacle is left standing,

Hebrews 10:18-20 Where there is forgiveness such as this, there's no longer a need for any sin offering. Therefore, brothers, we [should] have confidence to enter the holy place by the blood sacrifice of Jesus, by the new and living way initiated for us through the veil of His flesh.

and also to symbolize that even with the (continuous) offering of gifts and sacrifices, the worshiper is still not made perfect in his conscience,

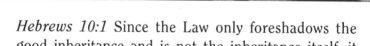

Hebrews 10:1 Since the Law only foreshadows the good inheritance and is not the inheritance itself, it can never be the (legal) instrument to make perfect those who draw near to God by the same sacrifices year after year.

Hebrews 7:19 . . . A better hope came about, and through that hope, we come closer to God.

Since these regulations of food, drink, and washing are imposed on the body until such time as the Law is reformed.

Mark 7:5,14,15;18-21 The Pharisees and the scribes asked (Jesus), "Why don't Your disciples do as the elders of the Jewish faith and clean their hands before they eat?" Jesus called to the group and all the people who had gathered around to be near Him and said, "Listen to Me [closely] so you'll understand [the answer]: nothing outside a human being can make him dirty by ingesting it, but it's things that come out of a man that make him impure." Turning to his disciples, He said, "You don't understand either? Don't you see? Whatever goes into man from the outside doesn't make him dirty because it doesn't go into his heart but instead he ingests it, it goes into his stomach, and then he eliminates it." (We take this to mean, Jesus proclaimed that no food was unclean or off-limits.) ". . . But out of the heart come evil thoughts, immoral sex, theft, murder, adultery, coveting, wickedness, deceit, lust, envy, slander, pride, and foolishness. That's what makes a man unclean and impure—the things that go out."

Alternatively, when Christ appeared as a high priest of a good inheritance,

Hebrews 2:17 Christ of necessity had to be like His brothers in God so that He could be a merciful and faithful high priest, to make atonement, or reconciliation, with God for the sins of the people.

Revelation 21:7 "The one who overcomes shall inherit these things. I will be his God and he will be My son."

He entered through the greater and more perfect tabernacle that wasn't created by man.

Revelation 11:19 The temple of God that is in heaven was open, and there in His temple appeared the ark of His covenant accompanied with [crashes of] lightning and peals of thunder, an earthquake, and a huge hailstorm.

Revelation 15:5,8 After all this, I saw that the temple in heaven for the house of the Testament was opened. . . . And it was filled with smoke from God's glory and power. No one could enter the temple until the seven angels' seven plagues were complete.

Revelation 13:6 And (the beast) utters sacrilegious things against God, against God's name, and against God's house, that is, those who are housed in heaven.

Hebrews 8:2 A high priest [Christ] . . . is the minister in the sacred temple and in the true, real house of God, which the Lord set up–not man.

Revelation 14:17 . . . Another angel came out of the temple in heaven. . . .

II Corinthians 5:1 If our [house] on earth is torn down, God has a building for us, one [He] built to last forever in the heavens.

 e entered with His own blood, not the blood of goats and calves.

John 2:19-21 Jesus said, "Destroy this temple (referring to His body) and in three days I'll resurrect it." The Jews [standing around] said, "It took forty-six years to build this temple, and You're going to put it back together in three days?!" [But they didn't understand His meaning.]

Hebrews 13:12 Likewise, Jesus was made to suffer outside the gate so He could purify the people with His own blood.

Titus 2:14 (Christ Jesus) gave His life for us so that He could purchase us back to God, paying for every crime, and so He could purify a whole group of people who belong to Him, until they are crazy about doing good deeds.

Revelation 1:5 Jesus Christ, Who loves us and released us from our sins with His blood, is the faithful witness, the firstborn of the dead, and the ruler of the kings of the earth.

 e entered once and for all, obtaining eternal redemption.

Hebrews 5:9 (Christ) was perfected by God and became the source of *everlasting salvation* for all who obey Him through suffering.

Revelation 21:3 . . . A loud voice from heaven said, "Look now, God's house is among mankind and He shall live with man and they shall be His people; God Himself shall be in the middle of them[!]"

Revelation 22:5 There won't be a need for night. They won't need a lamp for light, not even the sun, because the Lord God will shed light on them, and they (Christ's servants) shall reign *forever and ever.*

Revelation 5:8-10 When [the Lamb] had taken the book, the four living creatures and the twenty-four elders prostrated themselves before the Lamb, each having a harp and golden bowls of incense, that are prayers of the saints. They sang a new song: "You are worthy to take the book and break its seals because You were killed.

And with Your blood, You purchased for God men from every family and every language and every race and every nation. You have made them a kingdom and priests to our God, and they will exercise sovereign power over the earth."

Revelation 1:6 We are His kingdom and priests to God, His Father. . . . May Christ be glorious and dominant forever and ever. Amen.

If the blood of goats and bulls and the ashes of the heifer sprinkled over the impure purify the body,

Leviticus 16:18,19 <u>God instructs Moses</u> ". . . Take a little each of the blood of the bull and the blood of the goat. . . . Sprinkle some of the blood on the altar . . . to cleanse it and consecrate it from the impurities of the sons of Israel."

Numbers 19:9 <u>God instructs Moses and Aaron as to what to tell the sons of Israel</u> 'The ashes of the heifer shall be deposited outside the camp in a clean place by a clean man, and the descendants of Israel shall guard it to use as purification of sin, as if it were holy water.'

ince Christ, through the everlasting Holy Spirit, offered Himself perfect to God;

I Peter 3:18 Christ Himself died for sin, one time for all time–[He], the just, for [us], the unjust. Although His body was put to death, He was made alive through the Spirit of God, and thus He can bring us near God.

 ow much more will His blood cleanse your conscience from things you did leading to death under the Law, so you may serve the living God?

Revelation 1:5 Jesus Christ . . . loves us and released us from our sins with His blood. . . .

Ephesians 5:2 The same way Christ loved you and gave His life for [you] as a sacrificial and fragrant offering to God, so you should walk in a like, loving manner.

Revelation 12:11 And (our brethren) overcame (Satan, the accuser) because of the blood of Christ the Lamb, and because of their words testifying [about Christ and Salvation], and because they were willing to give up their life [for this].

Jude 24:25 To Him be glory, majesty, control, and authority, the only God our Saviour, through Jesus Christ our Lord, Who is able to keep you from making mistakes so as to [ultimately] stand joyous and guiltless in His glorious presence.

Revelation 22:3 There shall no longer be any curse, and the throne of God and of the Lamb shall be in it (the "holy city, new Jerusalem"), and His bond-servants shall serve Him.

ince Christ's death took place for the atonement of sins committed under the Law (the first Testament),

Hebrews 10:28 Anyone who willfully ignored the Law of Moses died with no mercy based on testimony from two or three witnesses.

Revelation 5:9 They sang a new song: "You are worthy to take the book and break its seals because You were killed. And with Your blood You purchased for God men from every family and every language and every race and every nation."

Ephesians 5:2 The same way Christ loved you and gave His life for [you] as a sacrificial and fragrant offering to God, so you should walk in a like, loving manner.

Deuteronomy 32:43 Rejoice, O nations, along with His people, for He will avenge the blood of His [dead] servants, and will render vengeance on those who oppose Him, and will *pay the sacrifice* to make amends for His land and His own people.

 hen those who have been selected or tapped by God

Romans 8:29,30 He knew those [who love God] before they existed and shaped their destiny so they'd conform to be like His Son so that His Son would be only the first resurrected of many brothers. Those whom He predestined, He also called; He also justified; He also glorified.

Romans 9:11,12 The twins (Jacob and Esau) had not done anything good or bad because they weren't even born yet. Based not on how they lived then, but in order to fulfill God's own choice and His own purpose, Rebekah was told: "The older (twin) will serve the younger."

Romans 11:25-29 Don't be wise in your own eyes. I don't want you to go uninformed: Israel has been partly hardened toward God's Word until all the Gentiles have come in [to the fold]. All of Israel will be saved, just as scriptures say: "The Deliverer will come from Zion and take away Jacob's ungodliness. This is My will for them, when I will absolve them of their sin." They are enemies when viewed strictly in light of [the life and death of Jesus Christ], but that was for your sake [so you as a Gentile could know Christ]. But as far as viewing them from the standpoint of what God chooses, He cherishes them on behalf of their ancestors. The gifts of God and the calling of God [in this context to the Jews] cannot be revoked.

ay receive the
everlasting inheritance,
which is God's promise.

Revelation 5:9,10 ". . . You were killed. And with Your blood, You purchased for God men from every family and every language and every race and every nation. You have made them a kingdom and priests to our God, and they will exercise sovereign power over the earth."

Revelation 21:7,4,6 "The one who overcomes shall inherit these things: . . . there shall no longer be any death nor therefore any mourning, nor crying, nor pain. . . . I will give from the very [well-] spring of the water of [eternal] life to the person who is thirsty for it—and he will pay nothing. . . . I will be his God and he will be My son."

Revelation 3:21 <u>Christ telling John what to write</u> 'I will grant to the one who overcomes the right to sit down with Me on My throne, since I also overcame and sat down with My Father on His throne.'

Revelation 22:12-15 "Look out, listen! I'm coming fast with My rewards to each man for his efforts. I am the Alpha and Omega, the first, the last, the beginning and the end." Those who cleanse themselves are blessed in that they will have the right to the tree of life and to enter the (holy) city [*new Jerusalem*]. Outside the city are the sodomizers and those who practice witchcraft and the immoral persons and murderers and those who worship false gods and everyone who loves and makes a practice of lying.

For this reason (His self-sacrifice), He is the mediator of a new contract between God and man [God's new Will and Testament].

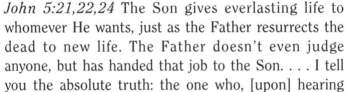

John 5:21,22,24 The Son gives everlasting life to whomever He wants, just as the Father resurrects the dead to new life. The Father doesn't even judge anyone, but has handed that job to the Son. . . . I tell you the absolute truth: the one who, [upon] hearing what I say, believes God (Who sent Me), will live forever, passing out of death into [the] life.

Galatians 3:17,18,29 What I am saying is this: the Law, which came four hundred and thirty years later [through Moses], didn't invalidate God's Will and Testament, so as to void the promise [of inheritance]. Look at it this way, if inheritance is based on law, then it's not based on a promise, but we know God granted [the inheritance] to Abraham through promise. If you belong to Christ, then you, yourself, are one of Abraham's children and therefore will inherit the promise.

Revelation 22:1-5 He showed me a river flowing with the water of life, bright as crystal, coming from the throne of God and of the Lamb in the center of its stream. On each side was the tree of Life with twelve crops of fruit, yielding fruit every month. And the leaves of the tree of Life were for healing the nations. There shall no longer be any curse, and the throne of God and of the Lamb shall be in it (the "holy city, new Jerusalem"), and His bond-servants shall serve Him. And they will look on His face, His name [always on their mind] emblazoned on their foreheads. There won't be a need for night. They won't need a lamp for light, not even the sun, because the Lord God will shed light on them, and they (Christ's servants) shall reign forever and ever.

I Timothy 2:5 There is one God, also one mediator between God and mankind, the man Christ Jesus.

Where there is a will, the one who makes it has to die [for the contractual will to be enforced].

It's, of course, never in effect while the one who made it lives, since a Will and Testament is only valid when death occurs.

That's why even the first Will and Testament was not put into effect without death.

 oses first told all the commandments to the people.

Exodus 24:3 Moses came to the people and told them everything the Lord (YHWH) had said to him, including the commandments, and the people said with one accord, "We will do everything the Lord has told us to do."

Exodus 34:31,32 Moses called out to them, so Aaron and the ones in authority with the congregation came back so he could speak to them. Later, all the sons of Israel came by and Moses commanded that they do everything the Lord had commanded him on Mount Sinai.

Then according to what the Law said, he took the blood of the calves and goats with water and red wool and hyssop and sprinkled both the book

Exodus 24:6,7 Moses put half the blood in basins and sprinkled the other half on the altar. Then he took the book of The Will and Testament and read it out loud to the people, who said, "We'll do anything God wants. We'll obey him."

(in which he had written all of God's words to him) and the people,

aying: "This is the blood of the Will and Testament by which God commanded you."

Exodus 24:8 Moses sprinkled some blood on the people, saying, "This is the blood of God's Will and Testament for you, with the promises He has made you [all written down]."

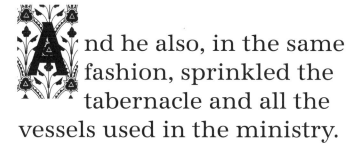

And he also, in the same fashion, sprinkled the tabernacle and all the vessels used in the ministry.

Exodus 40:9 "You shall anoint the house (tabernacle) for the ark of the Testament and everything in it and all its furnishings; set it apart for God as holy."

Leviticus 8:15 Next, Moses slaughtered (the bull sin offering) and with his finger dabbed its blood on to the horns of the altar to purify the altar, and then he poured out the blood at its base to set it aside as holy and make amends for it.

Leviticus 8:10 Moses then took the anointing oil and anointed the dwelling place [of the ark of the Testament] and set it aside, with everything in it, as holy.

Exodus 30:25-30 "Make it a holy anointing oil, as a fine perfume, with which you shall anoint the meeting tent and the ark of the Testament, and the table, its utensils, the lampstand and its utensils, and the altars of incense and burnt offerings and all their utensils, and the wash bowl and stand. Consecrate [set apart as holy] all of these so they are holy, and whatever touches them shall also be holy. Anoint also Aaron and his sons; set them apart as holy to minister to Me as priests."

Leviticus 16:14,16,18,32-34 "Finally, with his finger he shall sprinkle some of the blood of the [sacrificed] bull on the mercy seat on the east side and seven times in front of the mercy seat. . . . In this way, he shall make atonement for the holy place because of the impurities and sins of the sons of Israel and for the meeting tent as well, which is impure because their impurities are at its center. . . . After that, he shall go out to the altar of the Lord (YHWH) and make

atonement for it, and take a little each of the blood of the bull and the blood of the goat, and dab it on the horns of the altar on each side. . . . The priest, who is anointed and ordained to serve in his father's place [as his father before him did], shall put on the holy linen garments and make atonement for the holy sanctuary, the meeting tent, and the altar; he shall also make atonement for the [Levite] priests and for all the people gathered there. Now this is a permanent statute to make atonement for the sons of Israel for all their sins once every year." And Moses did exactly as the Lord commanded.

S o according to the Law, almost all things are made clean (purified) with blood, and without death and bloodshed there is no inherited forgiveness.

Leviticus 17:11 "The blood is the very life of the body, and I have allowed you to give it up on the altar to ask forgiveness and make amends (atone) for your souls. It is the blood itself, on behalf of the soul, that makes atonement."

Therefore, it was necessary for our earthly copies of heavenly things to be cleansed with these [types of death and sacrifices].

Hebrews 8:5 But they only symbolize and foreshadow the real heavenly things. Moses was even warned by God when he was ready to erect the tabernacle: "Be sure that you make all things by the pattern I showed you on the mountain."

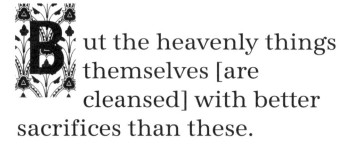

ut the heavenly things themselves [are cleansed] with better sacrifices than these.

Matthew 26:28 <u>Jesus speaking to his disciples at the Passover supper</u> ". . . This is the blood of the Testament, which is poured out on behalf of many, whose sins shall be forgiven."

Luke 22:20 Then He took the cup after they had eaten and said, "This cup represents My blood poured out for you that creates God's new will for mankind."

Christ did not enter a holy place created by man, but entered into heaven itself to appear in front of God for us.

John 7:33 Jesus told them, "I am with you for just a little longer, then I go [back] to the One who sent Me here."

Luke 9:51 He resolutely set about to travel to Jerusalem when it came close to time for Him to return to God.

Mark 16:19 After the Lord Jesus had spoken (to His eleven disciples), He was received by heaven and sat down at God's right hand.

John 6:62 Jesus speaking to disciples before some fell away, leaving just the twelve "What of it, if you see the Son of Man returning to heaven where He was before?"

John 20:17 Jesus said to Mary Magdalene ". . . Go to My brothers and tell them I am returning to Heaven to My Father and your Father, My God and your God."

John 16:28 <u>Jesus speaking to His disciples</u> "I started from the Father and came to the inhabited earth, which I will leave again to go back to the Father."

John 12:23 <u>Jesus speaking to Philip and Andrew</u> "The hour has come for the Son of Man to be made glorious."

Psalm 110:1 <u>David prophesying regarding the Christ</u> The Lord (YHWH) said to my Lord: "Sit at My right hand, until I make Your enemies a footstool for Your feet."

Matthew 26:64 Jesus answered (the high priest), "You said it, [I am the Christ, the Son of God]. But after this, you'll see the Son of Man sitting to the right of Power and coming [here] on heaven's clouds."

Isaiah 53:11,12 As a result of the suffering of His soul, He will see all this and be satisfied. The Righteous One, My Servant, will justify many with His knowledge [of God and man], as He will bear the guilt of man's sins. Therefore, I will allot Him a portion with the great, and He will divide the takings with the mighty because He gave of Himself even to death, being numbered with the sinners. He Himself bore the guilt of many and interceded for the real sinners.

Isaiah 54:5 "Your Creator is your husband, Whose name is 'the Lord of angels'. And your Saviour is the Holy One of Israel, Who is called 'the God of the whole earth.'"

Daniel 7:13-14 The Son of Man was presented before the ancient of days (God) and was given glory and rule over a kingdom. His control will last forever. His kingdom won't be destroyed.

And He doesn't have to enter it continually, each year, as the high priest enters the holy place.

Leviticus 16:34 "Now this is a permanent statute to make atonement for the sons of Israel for all their sins once every year." And Moses did exactly as the Lord commanded.

Otherwise, He would have needed to suffer many times since the beginning of the world;

Isaiah 53:2-10 Isaiah prophesying about the Christ He grew up before God like a tender [sucker] sprout arising from the root out of parched earth. He was not majestic or stately that we would be attracted to Him. He was despised and deserted, sad and surrounded by sickness. We were embarrassed to look at Him, much less acknowledge His greatness. He bore our own griefs Himself, and our sadness weighed on Him; yet we thought He was afflicted of God. He was wounded for our sins. He was put down and crushed due to *our* own imperfection. It fell upon Him to *purify us* for our own well-being, and by His being thrashed, we are healed. He took on the discipline meant for us. We were the ones that went our own way, wandering off from God, but He took our guilt all on Himself. He was oppressed and afflicted and still He didn't say a word. Like a lamb led to slaughter and a sheep silent before its shearers, He didn't utter one word. He was judged and tyrannized by unjust use of force before being taken away. Who in His generation would ever have

thought that He was killed for the sins of my people, who themselves deserved the hit? His grave was assigned with practicing sinners, yet [He received one] with a rich man at His death although He had committed no violence, nor was there any deceit in His words. The Lord (YHWH) was pleased to crush Him, putting Him to great sorrow. If He put Himself up as a guilt offering, He will see His children. He will extend His life; His hand will perform the pleasure of the Lord (YHWH).

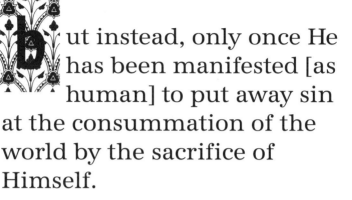

ut instead, only once He has been manifested [as human] to put away sin at the consummation of the world by the sacrifice of Himself.

<u>At the consummation of the world</u>

Isaiah 53:11-12 As a result of the suffering of His soul, He will see all this and be satisfied. The Righteous One, My Servant, will justify many with His knowledge [of God and man], as He will bear the guilt of man's sins. Therefore, I will allot Him a portion with the great, and He will divide the takings with the mighty because He gave of Himself even to death, being numbered with the sinners. He Himself bore the guilt of many and interceded for the real sinners.

Isaiah 24:4-6;21,23 The earth sadly withers and fades. The exalted people of the world fade away. The earth is polluted by its inhabitants. They break laws and ordinances and they broke their everlasting agreement with God [to take care of the earth–Genesis 1:28]. Therefore, the earth is cursed through its guilty inhabitants. Therefore the inhabitants of the earth are burned, except for a few.

In that day, the Lord (YHWH) will punish the angels and the rulers of the earth. Then the moon will not show, nor the sun. For the Lord of angels will reign on Mount Zion and in Jerusalem and will be glorious.

Isaiah 65:17; 66:22-24 "Look, I create new heavens and a new earth, and everything that existed in the past will be totally forgotten. Just as the new heavens and new earth that I make will be durable, your children and name will also endure from month to month, year to year. All of earth's inhabitants will be humble and worship Me," the Lord (YHWH) said. "And then they'll look out and see all the dead bodies of the rebels because those who rebel against Me will [not be allowed to rest in peace], and they'll burn non-stop, and all of mankind will be disgusted and horrified by their corpses."

Isaiah 50:4-10 "The Lord God (YHWH) gave Me the language of [My] disciples so that with a word I knew how to shed hope for the tired and depressed. He wakes Me each morning so I will listen and learn and follow. I did what He asked and completed My task. I gave My back to those who struck Me and My cheeks to the ones who plucked out My beard. I was spit upon and humiliated, but I didn't cover My face. For none other than the Lord God (YHWH) is My help. Therefore, [don't look for Me to be] disgraced; I've set My face like stone because I won't be ashamed. God, who vindicated Me, is close. You want to fight Me? Come on, stand up to Me. You have a case against Me? Come on, close in. The Lord God (YHWH) helps Me, and *you* are going to condemn Me?! Those [who rebel] will be eaten by moths and wear thin and wear out. Those of you who respect God and obey the Word of His Servant [Christ], but stumble around in the dark, [just] trust in the Lord [YHWH]'s name and rely on His God."

Isaiah 51:4-8 "Listen to Me, My people [body of believers], and listen to Me, My nation [Israel], I am going to bring justice as a light to the countries with My Law. My perfect goodness is close by and My salvation has begun. My arms will judge the countries; the coastal countries will look forward to My judgment. Look up at the sky, then down at the earth. The sky will vanish like a puff of smoke. The earth will wear out like a garment. And earth's inhabitants will die likewise. But My salvation shall be forever. My goodness shall never be lessened. Those of you who know My perfect goodness and on whose heart is My Law, listen to Me now. Don't worry about the ones taunting you or let their negativity upset you. They'll be eaten by moths and larvae, while perfection shall be forever, and I'll save all generations [from their sin]."

<u>By sacrifice (Jesus speaking)</u>

Matthew 20:28 "... The Son of Man did not come so [you could] serve Him, but as a servant, Himself, and to pay the ransom price for many lives with His own."

Mark 10:45 "The Son of Man did not even come to be served, but to be a servant, and give up His life as a ransom for many [souls]."

<u>Redemption from death—Christ as Saviour</u>

Isaiah 41:14 "Don't be afraid, sons of Jacob, men of Israel; I'll help you," the Lord (YHWH) states emphatically. "Your Saviour is the Holy One of Israel." [Note: Holy One of Israel is the Messiah/Christ.]

Isaiah 60:16 "You will be fed and mothered by nations and fathered and babied by kings. Finally you will know that I, (YHWH), am your Saviour and also your Redeemer, the same 'Mighty One' of Israel."

Isaiah 59:15-20 There's no truth anywhere, and the one who isn't evil becomes prey to those who are. The Lord was extremely upset that there was no justice, and He saw and was astounded that there was no man who could intervene in this. So His own [right] arm brought salvation to Him and His own perfection and goodness lifted Him up. He armored His bosom with perfection and goodness and His head with the knowledge of salvation. He wore vengeance into battle; He fought the elements with the heat of His zeal. He will repay furious anger to those who battle Him and to those who are His enemies. From east to west and along the coastlines, they will respect the name, Lord (YHWH). His wind will drive Him like water through a narrow stream. "One Who will recover My people with a price will come to Zion, to those in Israel who turn away from sin," He says.

It's appointed for man to die once and afterwards face judgment.

Dust to dust

Genesis 3:19 "You shall work hard for your bread until you return to the earth. Because I took you from the earth, you'll go back to dust from which I made you."

Psalm 90:3 You, (God), turn man back into dust, saying, "Return, child of mankind."

Psalm 104:29,30 When You turn away, (God), You disappoint them. They die when You take their breath; they return to earth's dust. Yet when You breathe Your Spirit, You create them, and thus rejuvenate the dust from the earth.

The period of judgment

I John 4:17 Since God lives in us and God is love, His love is perfected in us. By that, we should be confident in the period of judgment because we are in His love in the world.

Matthew 12:36,37 <u>Jesus speaking</u> "Every [evil] word that a man speaks will be accounted for in the [period] of judgment. By your own words, you shall be justified or condemned."

II Peter 2:9 . . . The Lord knows good and well how to rescue the man of God from tests and trials and how also to keep the ungodly under punishment for the [period] of judgment.

ikewise, Christ, Who suffered once for the sins of many, shall appear a second time, and not that time to bear sin,

Matthew 25:31,32,34,41 <u>Jesus speaking</u> "When the Son of Man comes [back] in all His glory along with the angels, He will at that time sit on His glorious throne. He will separate out the [peoples of the] nations that will come to Him, like a shepherd separates sheep from goats. . . . Then the King (the Son of Man) will say to (the sheep) on His right, 'You who are blessed [to know] My Father, come here; inherit the kingdom [We] have been preparing for you since [We] started creating the world.' . . . Then He will say to [the goats] on His left, 'You're cursed; get away from Me and into the fire that burns forever, prepared for the devil and his angels.'"

Mark 8:38 <u>Jesus speaking</u> "Whoever is ashamed of Me and of My Words in this adulterous age, the Son of Man will likewise be ashamed of him when He comes in glory from His Father with the holy angels."

but to [judge] those who eagerly wait for Him for their salvation.

Hebrews 13:14 We don't have a lasting city here, but we do look for the city [Zion, the new Jerusalem] which shall come.

Revelation 1:17-19 When I saw Him, I fell at His feet like a dead man. He laid His right hand on me and said, "Don't be afraid; I'm the first and the last and the Living One; I died, but now, see, I am alive forever, and I have the keys to death and hell. Write down all the things you've seen and what you're seeing now and what you will see after these."

Revelation 3:21 <u>Christ telling John what to write</u> 'I will grant to the one who overcomes the right to sit down with Me on My throne, since I also overcame and sat down with My Father on His throne.'

Revelation 7:14-17 . . . [The elder] answered, "These came out of the great time of suffering and distress; they have cleaned their robes [bright] white in the

blood of the Lamb. Therefore, they stand in front of God's throne and serve Him around the clock in His temple; and the One Who sits on His throne takes them into His house. They shall never be hungry or thirsty again, nor will the heat or the sun bear down on them. The Lamb, at the center of the throne, shall shepherd *them* and guide them to the springs of the waters of life; and God shall wipe every tear away from their eyes."

Revelation 14:7 ". . . Fear God, give Him glory; the hour of His judgment has come. Worship Him Who made the heaven, earth, sea, and springs of waters."

Revelation 19:9-16 He told me, "Write: 'Those who are invited to the wedding dinner of the Lamb are blessed.'" And he continued to say, "These are true words from God." I fell to (the angel's) feet to worship him, and he said, "Don't do that. *I am a fellow servant* with you and your brothers who hold the testimony of

Jesus–that is the spirit of prophecy. Worship God." I saw heaven open up and was looking at a white horse. The One Who rode it is called Faithful and True. He judges and conducts war in perfect goodness. His eyes are lit up by fire and on His head rest many crowns. No one knows the name written on Him, but Himself. He wears a robe dipped in blood. His name is "The Word of God". Heavenly Armies, clothed in clean white, fine linen followed Him on *their* white horses. A sharp sword [God's Word] comes from His mouth so that He can strike down the [rebellious] nations. He'll rule [with tough discipline] with a rod of iron; and makes wine [for them to drink] of the fierce anger of God, the Almighty [One].

Revelation 20:4-6 I saw (the twenty-four elders) [who sat down] on their thrones, having been given the authority to judge. And there were the souls of the people who had been beheaded because they were telling about Jesus, The Word of God. There were also

the souls of the people who did not [accept] the mark of the beast on their hand or forehead and of the ones who had not worshiped the beast. These all came to life and had supreme power with Christ for [an epoch of] a thousand years; this was the first resurrection. Everyone else stayed dead during that one thousand years until that epoch was finished. The one who is in that first resurrection is holy and blessed, for they are untouchable for the second death, and they'll be priests [serving] God and Christ and be given supreme power with Him [Christ] for [an epoch of] a thousand years.

Revelation 21:6-8 He said to me "It's done. I am the Alpha and Omega, the beginning and end. I will give from the very [well-] spring of the water of [eternal] life to the person who is thirsty for it—and they pay nothing. The one who overcomes shall inherit these things. I will be his God and he will be My son. As for the coward-hearted and non-believers and detestable murderers and immoral persons and those who practice

witchcraft and worship false gods and all liars, their
part will be in the burning lake with fire and
brimstone, which [for them] is the second death."

Revelation 22:12-17 "Look out, listen! I'm coming fast
with My rewards to each man for his efforts. I am the
Alpha and Omega, the first, the last the beginning and
the end." Those who cleanse themselves are blessed in
that they will have the right to the tree of life and to
enter the (holy) city [*new Jerusalem*]. Outside the city
are the sodomizers and those who practice witchcraft
and the immoral persons and murderers and those who
worship false gods and everyone who loves and makes
a practice of lying. "I am Jesus, Who has sent My angel
to tell you these things for [the sake of] the churches. I
am [both] the root and the offshoot of David; I am the
brilliant morning star." Then the spirit and the bride
[the holy city of Jerusalem; Zion, the new Jerusalem–vs
21:9,10] beckoned, "Come." The person who hears [and
understands] [these words] should also beckon,

"Come." So the one who is [parched and] thirsty [for eternal life], come and drink the water of [the everlasting] life at no expense.

I John 5:20 We know that the Son of God has come [to the world] and has imparted understanding so that we can know God is true and be part of the true God and His Son, Jesus Christ.

II Peter 3:9-15 Don't think the Lord is being slow. The Lord is patient with you, as He doesn't want anyone to die [the second death] and wants everyone to say they're sorry and ask forgiveness and turn away from their sinning. The day of the Lord [is going to sneak up on you] like a thief. With a roar, the heavens [above you] will fade from sight, and earth's elements will be destroyed by intense heat that man has made, and the earth itself will be burned up. Since everything is going to be destroyed, how should you conduct your life so as to be godly and holy? [Should you] look forward to the

Lord's day, when the heavens will be destroyed by burning and the elements will melt because of the intensity of the heat, and say: "Hurry up, hurry up"[?] Based on His promise, we look forward to new heavens and a new earth filled with what is right and good. So [the answer is], dear ones, you should be peaceful, pure, and not guilty. Be careful so you'll be found this way. Look at the patience of our Lord as being critical to our salvation, just as our dear brother Paul does, who has written to you in wisdom given by God.

I John 5:4-6;10-13 Whatever God conceived and gave birth to does overcome the [burdens of the] world. Our faith is victorious over the [burdens of the] world. So the one who has victory overcoming is the person who believes that Jesus is the Son of God. This (Jesus) came in water and blood, not just in water, but in water and in blood. . . . The person who believes in the Son of God has [received] the witness, but the person who does not believe the witness God gave concerning

[Christ] His Son, is calling God a liar. What the Spirit and water and blood attest to is that God has given us everlasting life in His Son. The person who belongs to the Son has the life; the one who does not belong to the Son of God does not have the life [Note: vs 11–"the life" refers to eternal life]. I have written these things to you who believe in the very name, "The Son of God", so you'll know that you will live forever [with Christ].

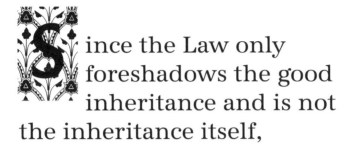

Since the Law only foreshadows the good inheritance and is not the inheritance itself,

Romans 5:13 A person is not charged with sin without law, even though sin existed in the world before the [Mosaic] Law [was given].

Luke 17:10 When you do everything commanded you [by God], [you need to think of it this way:] we have done only what we were supposed to do, as we are unworthy [even as] slaves [of God].

Exodus 25:8,9,40 Lord speaking to Moses "Allow them to build a sanctuary for Me, so I can live among them. Construct it just the way I'll show you and use that as a pattern for the house [in which I shall dwell] and the furniture for it. . . . Be sure you make them from the pattern you were shown on the mountain."

Acts 7:44 "Our ancestors in the wilderness had the house that God directed Moses to make for the Testament from the pattern God had shown him."

Exodus 31:15-17 <u>Moses to say to all Israel</u> 'Work may be done for six days, but there is a sabbath of complete rest on the seventh day that is holy to the Lord (YHWH). Whoever works on the sabbath shall be put to death. The sons of Israel shall observe the sabbath to celebrate the day of peace and rest throughout their generations as a perpetual agreement. It is a sign between Me and the descendants of Israel forever, because in six [epoch] days the Lord (YHWH) made heaven and earth, but on the seventh day He ceased from labor and refreshed Himself.'

Ezekiel 1:6;9;11;14-19;22-28 <u>Describing real heavenly cherubim, as opposed to the gold cherubim above the mercy seat</u> They had four faces and wings each, . . . their wings touched one another; their faces didn't turn, but were straight forward whenever they moved. . . . Their wings were spread out above them; two touched another [cherubim] and two covered their bodies. They ran back and forth like lightning. Now

that I'm looking, there were four wheels on the ground,
one for each [cherubim]. Each wheel looked the same,
as if it were a wheel within a wheel, and they looked
like they were crafted from beryl. Wherever they went,
in any direction, they would go without turning to
move. The rims were high and awesome and all the way
around they were covered with [something like] eyes.
The wheels went with the [cherubim] wherever they
went. When they rose, the wheels rose, too. There was
a kind of expanse, something like crystalline ice over
the heads of these living beings. And below this [you
could see] their outstretched wings, straight out,
touching each other, then the two wings covering their
body. From above the (crystalline ice) expanse, you
could hear a voice, and when the [cherubim] stood still
they dropped their wings. Above the expanse there was
something like a throne with the appearance of lapis,
and on it sat a figure that looked like a man. I saw from
His upper thigh upward something like a fiery
amber and below, something like fire; and there was

such a radiance surrounding Him. The aura looked like a rainbow surrounding Him. This is how the likeness of the glory of the Lord (YHWH) appeared. I fell on my face when I saw it and heard a loud voice speaking [to me].

t can never be the (legal) instrument to make perfect those who draw near to God by the same sacrifices year after year.

Jesus foreshadows God

John 12:44-46 Jesus yelled out, "The person who has faith in Me, has faith in the One Who sent Me. And the person who looks at Me, sees the One who sent Me. I have come to the world to light [the way to God], so that the person who has faith in Me won't stay in the dark [about God]."

John 13:20 Jesus speaking "The person who is receptive to My messengers is receptive to Me and the One Who sent Me."

Jesus's deeds foreshadow future gifts of men

John 14:11-12 Jesus speaking "Believe Me when I say I am in the Father and He is in Me. If you don't believe [this] because I say it, then believe it based on My actions and accomplishments. I tell you in all truth, the person who does have faith in Me will accomplish

things that I've done and greater things, because I'm
going [back] to the Father."

John 15:1-2;4-6;16 <u>Jesus speaking</u> "My Father feeds,
prunes, and trims My vine—I am the vine. Each of My
branches that doesn't bear fruit, He saws it off; but each
one that does, He prunes so it will bear even more fruit.
. . . Live in Me as I live in you; for just as the sawed off
branch cannot bear fruit severed from the vine, neither
can you, unless you live in Me. I am the vine and you
are the branches; the person who lives in Me, and in
whom I also live, will bear a lot of fruit. But severed
from Me, you can't do anything. If you do not live in Me,
you will be discarded like the branch and will dry up.
The dry branches will be gathered and thrown into the
fire and burned. . . . I chose you and selected you for
this time and place to bear fruit that would remain. You
did not choose Me. I have established that whatever you
ask of the Father in My name, He would give you."

John 17:24-26 <u>Jesus praying</u> "Father, I desire that they whom You gave to Me be with Me where I am, so they may behold My glory bestowed by You, for you have loved Me *before the foundation of the world* was laid. Father, you are [all that's] good and pure. I know You, even though earth's inhabitants do not. These, (My disciples), *do* know that You sent Me. I have and will continue to keep Your name [in front of them], so that they may be filled with Your same love for Me and [keep Me in their hearts]."

John 11:25 "I am the resurrection and the life [as spoken in prophecy]; even those who die shall live if they put faith in Me."

John 5:24 "I tell you the absolute truth: the one who, [upon] hearing what I say, believes God (Who sent Me), will live forever, passing out of death into [the] life."

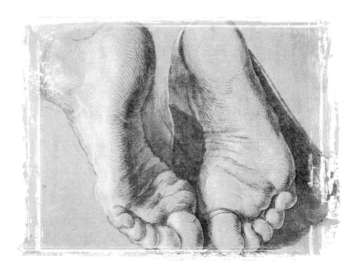

John 3:16,18,19 "God loved the peoples of the earth so much that He gave us the only Son He ever conceived, so that whoever put faith in His Son wouldn't die, but instead would live forever. . . . [Although] the one who has faith in Him isn't judged, the one who doesn't have faith in Him is judged [by his own lack of faith] in the only Son ever conceived by God. For He was God's enlightenment for men; however, [some] men don't wish to be illuminated, but rather love the darkness and do evil things."

Otherwise the worshippers, already purified, would no longer be aware of their sin and would quit making offerings.

Guilt as a result of awareness of sin

Exodus 28:42,43 "You must make (the priests) linen pants to cover their bottoms past their thighs, so they don't feel guilty when they come up to the altar in the meeting tent to minister in this place set apart for Me. . . ."

Genesis 3:11,22 Lord (YHWH) speaking to Adam "Who said you were naked? Who told you that? Did you eat fruit off that tree that I told you was absolutely off-limits?" . . . Then the Lord (YHWH) said, "Adam has become like Us, in that he now knows good from bad."

nstead, those sacrifices are there to be a reminder of sins year after year.

Exodus 29:42 "(The lamb) must be offered continually on down through the generations at the entrance to the meeting tent; so it will be there that I will meet you and speak to you."

Exodus 29:43-45 "I will meet at the entrance of the meeting tent [where the lamb is continually offered] with the sons of Israel. I will set apart for Myself the tent and the altar and Aaron and his sons to minister to Me as priest. And I will reside with the sons of Israel and be their God."

Exodus 23:14 "Three times a year you must have a feast on My behalf."

Numbers 15:28-30 'The priest must ask forgiveness and make amends to the Lord (YHWH) for the person who didn't know he was sinning so [I] may forgive him. Apply the same law to the naive sinner who's from Israel as to the naive sinner who's not. But it's different for the

person, whether from Israel or not, that sins defiantly. Because that person is being blatantly sacrilegious to God, he should (bear his guilt and) be removed from the people.'

Leviticus 16:34 "Now this is a permanent statute to make atonement for the sons of Israel for all their sons once very year."

Numbers 15:39-40 ". . . [Make] a tassel to look at so you'll remember to do all the commandments the Lord (YHWH) told you, instead of following your own eyes' and heart's desire; in this way you may set yourself apart [to serve] your God."

Romans 7:7 (Since we've been released from the Mosaic Law in order to serve God in the Spirit), shall we say that the Law itself is evil? No way! In fact, the [Mosaic] Law defines sin. [That's how we know what sin is.] How was I supposed to know what "coveting" or desiring another's possession is, unless the Law told me <u>not</u> to covet?

Because (after all) it's impossible for the blood of bulls and goats to [really] wipe out sin.

Romans 7:14 After all, the lamb *is* spiritual, but I'm of the [same] flesh [as Adam, who] sold [me] out to sin.

Romans 4:16 It is by faith along with grace that we become heirs so that the promise may be certain to all descendants—not just to those who are of the Law [the Jews]—but also to those who are of the faith [the Christian Gentiles] of Abraham (who is the father of us all).

Romans 8:1,2 No longer is there death for those who belong to Christ Jesus, because you have been set free from the law of sin and death by the law of the Spirit, which is life in the Christ, Jesus.

Psalm 32:1-5 My life blood went dry; I groaned day and night, while keeping my sin to myself. Your hand, (God), was [on my right shoulder], weighing me down. And I was sluggish and limp. [But when] I confessed my sin to You, (God), and didn't hide anything from

You, You forgave my sin and [obliterated] my guilt. The one whose sins are forgiven and buried is indeed blessed [by God]. How very blessed is the one who tells God the truth and whose guilt is not counted against him.

Thus when (Christ) comes into the world, He says, "Sacrifice and offering You did not desire, but You prepared a body for Me;

—Psalm 40:6

Luke 24:46,47 <u>Jesus explaining scriptural prophesy to his disciples</u> "It's written in prophesy that the Messiah would suffer, then rise from the dead on the third day. And (it is written) that these things should be declared officially to all countries, starting in Jerusalem: (1) repentance (or turning away from acting against God's rules), and (2) God's forgiveness of sins."

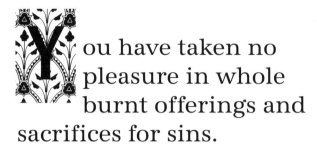

You have taken no pleasure in whole burnt offerings and sacrifices for sins.

—Psalm 40:6

Psalm 40:6-8 Sacrifice and grain offering You have not desired; You've opened My ears [to listen]. Neither have You required that they offer You burnt offerings or sin offerings. So I said, "Look, now I come, as it is written in scripture. I love to do Your will, My God. I carry Your law in My heart."

T hen I said, 'Look, now I have come (just as it is written about Me on the pages of the holy scripture) to do Your will, O God.'"

—Psalm 40:7,8

<u>Jesus speaking</u>

John 4:34 "What I live off of is doing what (the Father) wants Me to do and accomplishing His goals—that's where I get My nourishment."

John 6:38-40 "I was sent (by My Father) from heaven to do what *He* wants me to do (on earth), not so I could do what I want to do. What He wants is this: (1) that every one who looks at His Son and believes in Him will live forever, and (2) that I Myself will resurrect those same ones on the last [epoch] day, not losing any one that He gave Me."

After first saying "sacrifices and offerings" and then "whole burnt offerings and sacrifices for sin You did not desire, nor have You taken

[Compare to Leviticus 16, on pages 124-129.]

Pleasure in them" [in other words, speaking of the sacrifices offered to God according to the Law],

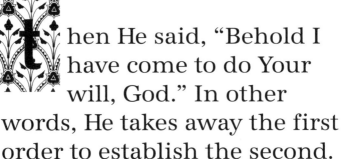

hen He said, "Behold I have come to do Your will, God." In other words, He takes away the first order to establish the second.

To do God's will

John 5:19,20 Jesus speaking "I tell you the absolute truth, [as] the Son (I) can't do anything on (My) own, unless it's something (I) see (My) Father doing. What He does, (I) copy. You know the Father loves the Son and therefore reveals to (Me) what He's doing. [What you saw] is only a sample of what He'll [do through Me] so you'll be in amazement."

Establishing the second order

John 5:21-24 (Jesus answered) "The Son gives everlasting life to whomever He wants, just as the Father resurrects the dead to new life. The Father doesn't even judge anyone, but has handed that job to the Son. And in so giving judgment, the Son will be honored by all [people and all] things—and if one doesn't honor the Son, that person dishonors the Father who sent Him. I tell you the absolute truth: the

one who, [upon] hearing what I say, believes God (Who sent Me) will live forever, passing out of death into [the] life."

John 8:31,32 Jesus said to the Jews who believed Him, "If you live by what I say, then you are My disciple; if you live by what I say, then you'll know the truth. [And sin will no longer be your Master], for the truth will set [your spirit] free."

y this (second, new order) we have been purified for God through the [sacrificial] offering of the body of Christ, once and for all time.

New order: forgiveness and resurrection to everlasting life

Luke 5:19-24 They let (the paralyzed man) down through an opening they made in the roof by taking off the tiles and set his stretcher right in front of Jesus. [Impressed] with their faith, He told the man, "Gentleman, you are forgiven for the sins you committed [against God]." The scribes' and Pharisees' [minds were racing]: "Who does this man think He is? He's uttering abominable things with regard to God— Who is *He* to forgive sins; only God can do that!" Jesus knew exactly what they were thinking, so He said to them, "[Don't question My authority.] I could as easily have said, 'Rise and walk', but just so you know the Son of Man has the power on earth to forgive sins, [I say to this man]," (he turned to the paralyzed man to address him), "I tell you, get up, take your stretcher and go home."

John 6:27-29 Jesus said, "Don't labor for food for your table; [it'll be there]; instead labor for the spiritual nourishment that I'll give you. God, the Father, has set His personal seal [of approval] on (the Son of Man), and the food I give you will sustain you forever." (His disciples) asked Him, "What kind of labor shall we perform [so we'll receive this spiritual food]?" Jesus said, "All God wants you to do is to believe in (the Son of Man) Whom God sent [to earth]."

John 6:44-49 <u>Jesus speaking</u> "No one can come to Me unless My Father who sent Me draws that one to Me; that person I will resurrect on the last [epoch] day. Everyone who has ever heard from and understood The Father [shall] come to Me [in resurrection], as it is written in the books of the prophets, 'They shall all be taught by God.' Of course, no man has seen the Father except the One Who is from the Father. But I am the food, giving life. Your ancestors ate manna in the wilderness and they died; but I tell you the absolute truth, the one who believes [in Me] will live forever."

<u>Sacrificial offering of the body of Christ</u>

Luke 9:22-24 <u>Jesus to His disciples</u> "The Son of Man must suffer and be rejected by the (Jewish) elders and head priests and scribes and then be killed, but He'll be resurrected on the third day. If any of you wants to follow in My footsteps, you must deny your personal desires and pick up the burdens of the world [and sacrifice yourself] for Me. I'll tell you, you're going to lose [the real everlasting] life if you want to keep living [in sin], but you will have [the everlasting] life if you give up your [sinful] life for My sake."

Roman 5:8 Christ's death on our behalf, sinners though we are, is God's demonstration of His own love for us.

Luke 22:19,20 He took some bread, and gave thanks, then broke it, and gave it to them, saying, "This is My body which I give up for you; do this to remember

Me." Then He took the cup after they had eaten and said, "This cup represents My blood poured out for you that creates God's new will for mankind."

hough the priests minister every day and offer the same sacrifices time after time, those sacrifices can never take away sins.

Romans 5:9 (Christ) poured out His blood for us to [make amends for our sins and purify us before God], so we could be saved from God's wrath through [our faith in His] Christ.

Romans 5:14 Death had power over men from Adam to Moses, even over the ones who had not sinned exactly like Adam. [Of course,] Adam was [the antithesis (or exact opposite reflection)] of the [Christ] Who was to come.

But Christ, having offered just one sacrifice for all sins for all time, sat down at God's right.

Romans 5:19 Just as through one man's (Adam's) disobedience many were made sinners, through the *obedience of the One (Christ)* many will be made righteous.

John 10:17,18 <u>Jesus speaking</u> "The Father loves Me because I shall sacrifice My life so that I may live again. No one takes My life, but I put it to rest on My own initiative. I have authority to lay My life down and authority to take it up again. *My Father commanded Me to do so.*"

And since then He has waited on the day "until all His enemies be made a footstool for His feet".

—Psalm 110:1

Psalm 110:1 The Lord (YHWH) says to my Lord: "Sit at My *right hand,* until I make Your enemies a footstool for Your feet."

y one offering, He has perfected those who are set apart for purification.

John 10:26-28 <u>Jesus speaking</u> "You are not one of My sheep, so you don't believe Me. I know My sheep, and when they hear Me calling them, they come follow Me. No one can snatch them away from the Father; they will never pass out of existence because I will give them everlasting life."

John 8:47 <u>Jesus speaking</u> "He who is of God hears the Words of God. You don't hear them, because you are not of God."

John 5:21-25 The Son gives everlasting life to whomever He wants, just as the Father resurrects the dead to new life. The Father doesn't even judge anyone, but has handed that job to the Son. And in so giving judgment, the Son will be honored by all [people and all] things—and if one doesn't honor the Son, that person dishonors the Father who sent Him. I tell you the absolute truth: the one who, [upon] hearing what I say and believes God (Who sent Me) will live forever,

passing out of death into [the] life. The truth is, the hour is upon us when the dead will hear the Son of God's voice and those who [listen and respond to it shall live forever].

he Holy Spirit also furnishes evidence to us because, after saying:

Ephesians 1:13 Once you heard the gospel truth and believed in your salvation in (Christ), [God] put His personal seal on you with the Holy Spirit He promised.

John 20:22 (Jesus) [(resurrected but not yet ascended to heaven)] breathed on (the disciples), "Receive the Holy Spirit."

Romans 9:1 Paul writes The Holy Spirit furnishes evidence to my conscience that I am not lying but am telling the truth in Christ.

Jesus speaking

Luke 11:13 ". . . Your Father in heaven [will] give the Holy Spirit to the ones who ask Him [for it]."

Luke 12:12 "The Holy Spirit will teach you what to say (in your own defense)."

John 14:26 "The Holy Spirit, or 'Helper', Whom the Father will send in My name, will teach you and help you *remember* everything I said."

This is the Will and Testament I will make with them at the close of the age, says the Lord:

Jeremiah 31:33 <u>God declared to Jeremiah, the prophet</u> "This is the Will and Testament that I will make for the house of Israel for later days," announces the Lord. "I will put My law inside them and write it on their heart. I will be their God, and they shall belong to Me."

2 Ezekiel 11:16-20 <u>God speaking through Ezekiel's prophesy about Israel</u> "The Lord says this, 'Although I scattered [the sons of Israel] out among the countries and moved them far [from their land] into many nations, I was still with them and a sanctuary to them in those places.' So, tell them I said this, 'I will gather you up from these various countries where you went and get you together and give you the land of Israel.' When they get to (the land of Israel) they'll get rid of all those things I hate—all the abominable things. I will give them a unified heart and a fresh spirit. I'll give them a soft heart to replace theirs that are [grown] stone [cold]. Then they'll walk in My law and they will be My people and I shall be their God."

I will put My laws upon their heart and upon their mind I will write them."

—Jeremiah 31:33

Jeremiah 24:7 The Word came to (Jeremiah): "Thus says the Lord God (YHWH) of Israel, 'They will know Me in their heart, as I am the Lord (YHWH). . . .'"

 e then says, "And their sins and their lawless acts I will forget."

—Jeremiah 31:34

Jeremiah 31:34 "They won't teach each other, saying, 'Know the Lord', because they'll all know Me, great and small," announces the Lord (YHWH), "because I'll forgive their impurity and forget their sin."

Isaiah 43:24,25 ". . . You have made Me tired of your burdensome sins. I am the very same One Who wipes out your sins—not for your sake, but for Mine. I mean, I won't even remember your sins."

Isaiah 38:17 <u>Hezekiah in prayer</u> . . . You (Lord) have put all my sins *behind me.*

Micah 7:7,9 . . . I expect the Lord (YHWH) to come, so I watch for Him and wait for Him, my Saviour. . . . The Lord (YHWH) will be upset with me for the things I've done wrong against Him. [But then,] He'll plead my case [before the throne] and *declare me not guilty.* He'll bring me [out of the darkness] into the light. And I will understand Him and understand His purity and goodness.

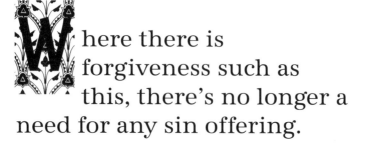 here there is forgiveness such as this, there's no longer a need for any sin offering.

Hosea 6:6 God speaking through His prophet, Hosea Loyalty and the knowledge of God make Me happier than sacrifices or burnt offerings.

Hebrews 9:27 . . . Only once has He been manifested (as human) to put away sin at the consummation of the world by the sacrifice of Himself.

Psalm 130:3,4 If you, Lord (YHWH), should keep track of each wrongful act against You, My Lord, who could stand?! But with You there's forgiveness, so You will receive respect.

Acts 13:38,39 "Know this, siblings in Christ: through Christ Himself, God has proclaimed His *forgiveness* of your sins. Through (Christ), everyone of you who *believes* is freed from all things by which you were enslaved under the Law of Moses."

Therefore, brothers, we [should] have confidence to enter the holy place by the blood sacrifice of Jesus,

Hebrews 9:22 "So according to the Law, almost all things are made clean (purified) with blood, and without death and bloodshed there is no inherited forgiveness.

Ephesians 1:7 Through (Christ's) blood we have been saved from death, forgiven of our sins against God.

Matthew 26:28 <u>Jesus speaking to his disciples at the Passover supper</u> ". . . This is the blood of the Testament, which is poured out on behalf of many, whose sins shall be forgiven."

Hebrews 9:24 Christ did not enter a holy place created by man, but entered into heaven itself to appear in front of God for us.

 y the new and living way initiated for us through the veil of His flesh.

Old way

Hebrews 9:7,8 But only the high priest, and he only once a year, enters into the second tabernacle (holy of holies), always taking blood to offer God for his atonement of sins and the sins of the people committed out of ignorance. The Holy Spirit is using this tabernacle structure to signify that the way to the holy place is not revealed as long as the first tabernacle is left standing.

New way

Hebrews 9:11,12 Alternatively, when Christ appeared as high priest of a good inheritance, He entered through the greater and more perfect tabernacle that wasn't created by man. He entered with His own blood, not the blood of goats and calves. He entered once and for all, obtaining eternal redemption.

ow we have a great [high] priest over the house of God.

Christ the great priest

Hebrews 2:17 Christ of necessity had to be like his brothers in God, so that He could be a merciful and faithful high priest, to make atonement, or reconciliation, with God for the sins of the people.

Over the house of God

Ephesians 2:19-21 . . . (You are) part of God's household–part of a building. Christ is the corner stone; the apostles and prophets form the foundation. When all are fitted together we become the temple of the Lord, set apart as the dwelling place of God in the spirit.

I Peter 2:5 Like living stones You are being built into a spiritual house for God's priesthood. This is in order that you may make spiritual sacrifices [pleasing] to God through Jesus Christ

II Corinthians 6:16 . . . We are the house of the living God, just as God said, "I will dwell in them and walk with them."–Leviticus 26:11,12

I Corinthians 3:16 Don't you know that you are the house for God and that God's Spirit lives inside you?

Hebrews 3:6 . . . As a body of believers, we belong to Christ. . . .

I Timothy 3:15 . . . The church of the living God . . . is the household of God, supporting the truth.

Jesus Christ's] sprinkled blood [sacrifice] has cleansed our hearts from their evil intentions; [His] purifying water [of life] has made ready our bodies [for God].

Faith

Hebrews 11:1 Faith is the conviction of our hopes and dreams.

Sprinkled clean

Ezekiel 36:25 <u>The Lord speaking of Israel</u> I will sprinkle you with clean water so you'll be clean. I'll cleanse you. . . .

I Peter 1:2 . . . Obey Jesus Christ and . . . be sprinkled with His blood. . . .

Cleansed with purifying water

Ephesians 5:26 (Christ) purified (the Church) [for God], cleansing her with the water of the Word.

[Since our hearts control our thoughts, which control our bodies,] be convicted by your faith, then, so you can approach God where He lives.

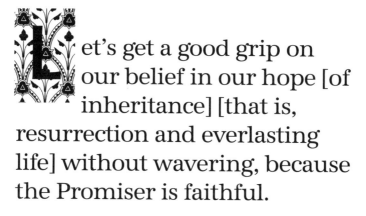 et's get a good grip on our belief in our hope [of inheritance] [that is, resurrection and everlasting life] without wavering, because the Promiser is faithful.

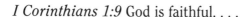

I Corinthians 1:9 God is faithful. . . .

Isaiah 49:6,7 <u>Isaiah prophesying about God's *Servant*</u> "It's not enough that You should be My Servant to resurrect the tribes of israel, to restore those [I have] preserved. I will also make You a light to the [Gentile] nations, so My salvation may cover all the earth. . . . Kings . . . and princes shall submit [to You] because of the Lord Who is faithful, the Holy One of Israel Who has chosen You.

I Thessalonians 5:24 The One Who called you is faithful—He will cause it to happen.

Acts 2:39 <u>Peter speaking</u> "The *promise* is for you and your children, even for [God's children] who are far away; it's for all those who the Lord God shall call to come to Him."

 et's figure out how to influence each other into love and good deeds,

II Timothy 2:24,25 As the Lord's bonded servant, [you] shouldn't be argumentative. Be kind to everyone and be patient when you've been wronged. Correct those who oppose you with gentleness . . . so you can teach them. God may [allow them to repent], which will lead them to knowing [and understanding] the truth.

II John 4 Since we had been commanded by the Father [to do so], I was delighted to see some of your children living their life according to the truth.

Titus 3:8 . . . Those who believe God [must] be careful to keep busy doing good deeds because good deeds profit mankind.

I Peter 5:14 Greet each other with a loving kiss.

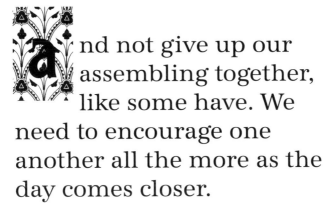

nd not give up our assembling together, like some have. We need to encourage one another all the more as the day comes closer.

Acts 2:42-44 They gave their complete attention to the teachings of the apostles [Christ's eleven disciples plus Matthias who replaced Judas Iscariot—Acts 1:26] and to fellowship [with each other], breaking bread and praying. Everyone was kept in awe by the signs and miracles performed through the apostles. The believers shared all things together.

Acts 1:14 (The apostles), all intent on the same things, gave constant attention to prayer, along with Mary the mother of Jesus, His brothers, and the women.

Hebrews 3:13 All day long encourage each other, day after day, so that not one of you will be hardened by sinful tricks and lies.

Philippians 2:2 . . . Be intent on one purpose, united in spirit, of one mind, holding the same love.

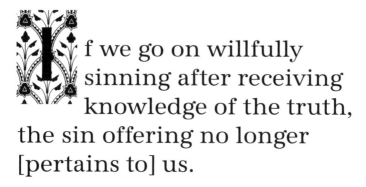

If we go on willfully sinning after receiving knowledge of the truth, the sin offering no longer [pertains to] us.

Numbers 15:30,31 . . . The person, whether from Israel or not, that sins defiantly . . . is being blatantly sacrilegious to God; he should (bear his guilt and) be removed from the people. Because he despised the Word of God and broke God's commandment, he shall remain guilty.

Matthew 12:45 . . . The state of that man becomes worse than at first. . . . And so will it be with this evil generation.

II Peter 2:20-22 If, after they have overcome the sins of the world by knowing of the Lord and Saviour Jesus Christ, they become entangled in and are overtaken by them again, this last situation is worse than the first.

Hebrews 6:4-6 In the case of a person who fell away after he or she was enlightened and experienced a heavenly gift of the Holy Spirit, who has also experienced the Good Word of God and has a sense of the powers of the coming age, it's impossible for man to convert them again, since they crucify Christ a second time for themselves and shame Him openly.

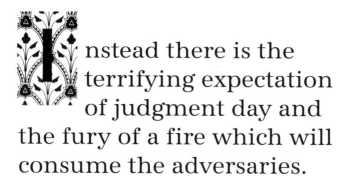

Instead there is the terrifying expectation of judgment day and the fury of a fire which will consume the adversaries.

Judgment

John 5:29 . . . Those who did good deeds (shall) rise to [everlasting] life and those who did evil deeds (shall) rise to judgment.

Jude 14,15 Enoch, in the seventh generation from Adam, prophesied, "Look, the Lord came with thousands and thousands of His holy ones to execute *judgment* on everyone, and to convict all the ungodly of all their ungodly acts done in an ungodly manner, and to convict the ungodly sinners who have spoken harsh things against Him."

Isaiah 26:21 Look now, because the Lord is about to come out to punish the inhabitants of the earth for their sins against God. The earth will be covered with the bloodshed of the slain.

Consuming fire

II Thessalonians 1:7 . . . [We shall see] Jesus [coming] from heaven with His mighty angels, surrounded with flaming fire.

Isaiah 26:11 Lord, . . . indeed, fire will engulf your opposition.

Isaiah 50:11 . . . All you who kindle a fire . . . [go ahead], walk in its light in the blaze you have set yourselves. This is what I give you: lie down [in it] and be tormented.

Revelation 19:20 The false prophet performed signs by the authority of the beast and thus he deceived those with the beast's mark (the same ones who idolized the beast's picture). So the false prophet was seized along with the beast and thrown alive into the lake of fire burning with scalding sulphur.

Revelation 20:14,15 The lake of fire is the second death. The god of the underworld [Satan] and death, itself, were thrown into the lake of fire, as was anyone whose name was not found written in the book of life.

Anyone who willfully ignored the Law of Moses died with no mercy based on testimony from two or three witnesses.

Deuteronomy 4-6 ". . . And if it is true and absolutely certain that this detestable thing has been done in Israel, then you shall bring out that man or that woman who has done this evil thing to your gates, and you shall stone them to death. On the evidence of two witnesses or three witnesses, that person shall be put to death; he shall not be put to death on the evidence of one witness."

How much more severe do you think the punishment will be for the person who treats the Son of God like dirt and

I Peter 4:17 It's time for judgment to begin, beginning with the household of God. If we [believers] are the beginning of judgment, what will happen to those of us who disobey the true account from God? And if it's so tough [for the believers] to be saved, what's going to become of the godless person and the sinner?

Matthew 18:16,17 If (your brother who has sinned and whom you have reprimanded) doesn't listen to you, then take one or two other with you to listen and confirm all the facts. If he doesn't listen to them either, then go to the church with the problem. If he refuses to listen to the body of believers, then let him be [despicable] to you.

regards the blood of Jesus
that validated His inheritance
with God as impure and,
further, has insulted the Holy
Spirit of Grace?

We know Who it was Who said, "Vengeance is Mine, I will repay," and also, "The Lord will judge His people."

−Deuteronomy 32:35 and Psalm 67:4

Deuteronomy 32:35 <u>Moses teaching Israel the words to his song</u> 'Vengeance is Mine and [I will] inflict impartial punishment. You will judge the peoples with perfect goodness.'

Genesis 18:25 <u>Abraham to the Lord (YHWH)</u> "Far be it from You (Lord) to slay the pure and good people right along with the wicked ones−to treat them the same. Far be it from You, Lord! Won't the Judge of [all] the earth deal fairly?"

Isaiah 44:22 I have wiped out your sins against me [that hung] like a heavy cloud of mist [between us]. Return to Me, for I have purchased you back for Myself.

t would be a terrifying thing to fall into the hands of the living God.

Psalm 50:22 ". . . Consider this, those of you who forget about God, in case I tear you into pieces and there's no one to deliver you."

Deuteronomy 32:22 <u>Moses teaching Israel the words to his song</u> 'My anger is like a kindled fire. It burns as far as the deepest part of hell and consumes the earth and its crops and its mountain cores.'

<u>The Lord, in John's vision, telling him what to write</u>

Revelation 2:16 'Turn back from sin, or else I am coming quickly. I will make war against [men] with the sword of My mouth [the Word of God].'

Revelation 22:12 "Look out, listen! I'm coming fast with My rewards to each man for his efforts."

Revelation 20:12 I saw the dead, the great, and the lowly standing before the throne, and books were opened, and another book was opened that is the book of life. Then the dead were judged from the things which were written in the books, corresponding to their deeds.

Remember the old days when after seeing the light (so to speak) you endured a great deal of suffering?

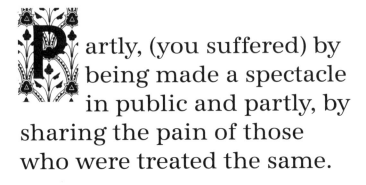

artly, (you suffered) by being made a spectacle in public and partly, by sharing the pain of those who were treated the same.

James 5:13 Are any of you suffering? Then you should pray.

I Peter 2:20,21 . . . When you do the right thing and suffer for it and patiently get through it, God looks with favor on that. . . . [Remember,] Christ also suffered [doing the right thing] for you [and endured], giving you a good example to follow.

II Timothy 2:3 Paul's letter to Timothy Suffer these difficult, painful conditions with me, as a good soldier [fighting] for Christ.

Philippians 4:14 Paul to the church in Philippi . . . You have done well, sharing my continuous suffering.

I Corinthians 4:9,10 We apostles have been put up by God to be a spectacle to the angels and men of this world, I think. We are condemned to death, but we are fools for Christ's sake. . . .

You showed sympathy to the prisoners and accepted the seizure of your property with happiness, knowing you had a better possession, an everlasting one.

<u>Sympathy to the prisoners</u>

Hebrews 13:3 Think of the prisoners, as if you were there with them, and also those who are treated badly since we all belong to the body (of believers in Christ) (for which they suffer).

Matthew 25:36 <u>Jesus speaking of what the king will say to those who inherit the kingdom</u> 'I had no clothes to wear and you gave Me some; I was ill and you came to see Me; I was in prison and you came to [minister] to me.'

II Timothy 1:16 <u>Paul writing to Timothy</u> Make the Lord grant forgiveness to Onesiphorus's household. He so often refreshed me while I was in prison and wasn't embarrassed by my chains.

The everlasting possession

Matthew 5:12 You should be excited! Your reward is great in heaven, as you follow the footsteps of the prophets who were persecuted, too.

Colossians 3:23,24 Whatever you do, do it from the heart like you're doing it for the Lord, rather than for men, knowing that you will receive the reward of inheritance from the Lord; it is Christ you serve.

I Peter 1:4 (God has caused us) to obtain an inheritance that can not be cut short, is totally pure, will not fade, and is reserved in heaven for you.

o don't throw away your confidence which has a great reward.

Romans 8:17 Now, if we are His children, then that makes us God's heirs also, *heirs along with Christ*; (if we suffer with Christ, [it's] so we may be given glory with Him).

Acts 20:32 . . . You shall be given the inheritance along with all those who are set apart for God through the Word of His salvation.

I Peter 5:4 When the Chief Shepherd comes, you will be crowned with a [halo] of glory that will shine brightly forever.

You need to endure, so that when you've done God's will, you may receive that (inheritance) He promised you.

Hebrews 12:1 . . . Let's set the sin aside that trips us up and run with endurance the race in front of us.

Matthew 10:22 All will hate you because of My name, *Christ*, but the one who endures [through it all] to the end will be saved [from death].

Matthew 24:11-14 <u>Jesus prophesying</u> There will be numerous lying prophets who will deceive many people. Most people will lose their love because anarchy [and terror] will increase. But the person shall be saved who endures [through it all] to the end. This true account of the kingdom [of God] will be preached to all the peoples of the earth as evidence [given to God's salvation].

For yet in a very little while, He Who is coming will come and will not delay. My righteous One shall live by faith.

<u>Saviour coming quickly</u>

Revelation 22:7 <u>John's vision</u> "Watch out! I am coming fast. The person will be blessed who pays attention to the prophetic words of this book."

Revelation 22:20 <u>John's vision</u> The One Who gave all of this testimony said "I am coming fast." Amen. Come on, Lord Jesus.

Psalm 96:13 . . . He is coming; (the Lord) is coming to judge the inhabited earth. With perfect, good, faithful judgment He will decide the fate of the earth and its people.

Psalm 43:11,12 I am the Lord (YHWH). There is no other Saviour except Me. I have told you that I would save you; I did save you, and I have proclaimed that [to the world]. . . .

The Righteous One and the faithful

Psalm 132:17,18 . . . I have [lit] a lamp for My Anointed One. His crown shall illuminate Him. His enemies will openly wear their shame.

Isaiah 53:11,12 . . . The Righteous One, My Servant, will justify many with his knowledge [of God and man], as He will bear the guilt of man's sins. Therefore, I will allot Him a portion with the great. . . .

Romans 1:16,17 . . . The true (gospel) story is [about] God's power in salvation to all who have faith–first to the Jews and then to the Greeks. In it the purity and goodness of God is revealed from one [account of] faith to another. It is written in the scriptures: "The righteous man shall live by faith."

ut [the one who] shrinks back, my soul has no pleasure in him."

—Habakkuk 2:3,4

Isaiah 9:13,17 ". . . The people don't turn back to [God], they don't seek out the Lord (YHWH) of angels. . . . Therefore the Lord has no pleasure in [them]. . . ."

Isaiah 57:20 . . . "There is no peace for the wicked," says God.

Isaiah 66:3,4 ". . . Because they have chosen their own ways [of sacrifice and worship, rather than God's] and they love despicable things, I will select their punishment [accordingly]. It will be [exactly] what they dread. I called [them] and they didn't listen or answer Me, but rather purposely did evil and made choices that [would] displease Me."

Isaiah 65:11,12 <u>The Lord said to Isaiah, His prophet</u> "Those of you who give up on the Lord (YHWH), who forget the [nation] I set apart for Myself, but set a place for Fortune and [celebrate] Destiny, I'll *destine you*–for the sword. You'll be subject to a slaughter, because I called you and you ignored Me. I spoke to you, but you didn't [want to] hear. You purposely did evil and made choices that would displease Me.

We are not the ones who will shrink back, just to be destroyed, but we are one of the group who have the faith that will preserve the soul.

Isaiah 63:8,9 He said, "Indeed they are My people, sons who will deal truthfully." So He became their Saviour and suffered all that they suffered. The angel of His [spirit] saved them . . . .

Psalm 37:10,11 Before long, there will be no wicked. You'll search all over for him, but he won't be there. The humble [in heart] will inherit the land and will be happy in their overwhelming prosperity.

Faith is when you are sure of things you hope for, though you have seen no evidence.

Romans 10:17 It is by *hearing*–(specifically) hearing the Word of Christ–that we obtain faith.

II Corinthians 5:7 We walk with faith as our guide rather than our eyes.

II Corinthians 4:18 . . . The things that we *can* see are just temporary. The things that we *can't* see are forever.

Romans 8:24,25 Why does anyone hope for what he can see? That's not *hope*. We hope for what we don't see, even eagerly wait for it. By this hope we've been saved.

y faith men through the ages gained (God's) approval.

By faith we understand that the worlds were created by the Word of God, so that what we see is made from things we can't see.

Faith in what we can't see

II Peter 3:5 ". . . By the Word of God the heavens existed a long time ago and . . . the earth was formed by and out of water."

John 1:1-3 The Word was in the beginning of all things. The Word was with God. The Word was, in fact, God. He was *with God* from the first. All things came to exist *through Him.* There is nothing in existence that began without Him.

Colossians 1:16 In Christ, all things in heaven and all things on earth were created, both the visible and the invisible. The seat of sovereign power, the power to rule, the law and its enforcement . . . have been created through Christ and for Christ.

By faith Abel offered God a better sacrifice than (his brother) Cain, so his offering was testimony to his righteous nature.

Abel's faith

Genesis 4:4,5,8,10 ". . . Abel and his offering made God happy. But God didn't like Cain or his offering . . . So Cain . . . killed his brother Abel. God said to Cain, "What in the world have you done?! Your brother's blood is crying to Me from the soil [where you killed him]."

God, Himself, testified about receiving Abel's gifts, so due to his faith, Abel still speaks to us even though he's dead.

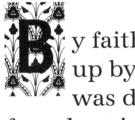 y faith Enoch was taken up by God before he was dead and wasn't found again.

Enoch's faith

Genesis 5:23,24 Enoch lived three hundred and sixty five years. He walked with God. Then God took him [and he was not found].

He obtained the witness that he was pleasing to God before he was taken up.

 ithout faith (on the other hand) it is impossible to please Him;

Faith that God exists, faith in God's rewards

Luke 18:17 I tell you the truth, in order to enter the kingdom of God, one must receive [the news of] it [with the same loyalty, curiosity, and pure joy] as a child.

Matthew 12:30 [Jesus said,] "The one who is not *with* Me is *against* Me, the one who doesn't [consciously] work with Me to gather [the sheep to the kingdom] is [actually] driving them away."

Matthew 13:44 Jesus's parable "You could compare the kingdom of heaven to a hidden treasure. When you discover it, you sell everything you have in order to obtain the *rights to the treasure.*"

Mark 5:30,33,34 Jesus sensed that His power had just been released and turned [swiftly] around. "Who touched me?" he asked. The woman (who had done it) was scared . . . and fell in front of (Jesus), confessing

for anyone who comes to God must believe that God exists and that He rewards the people who seek Him out.

[that it was she]. (Jesus) said to her, "Daughter [of the Father], you have [just] been *healed by your faith*. Go in peace."

Matthew 19:29,30 <u>Jesus speaking to His disciples</u> "Everyone who has given up their home or family or property because of [their faith in] Me shall be *rewarded many times over* and will inherit [the] everlasting life. Understand, however, that many who are first [to serve the Lord] will be last [to receive their reward] and the last [group to serve the Lord] will be [the] first [to receive their reward]. [Note: this timing is clarified in the parable of the vineyard labors in Matthew 20:1-16.]

Matthew 16:27 (Jesus said to His disciples) "[When] the Son of Man comes [back] in His Father's glory with His angels, [He] will *reward each person* what he is due according to his actions.

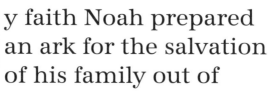

y faith Noah prepared an ark for the salvation of his family out of reverence for God, Who had warned Noah that He was about to destroy the world.

Noah's faith

Genesis 6:11,17,18,22,9 God saw that the earth was violent and corrupt . . . [thus He said to Noah], "I'm going to cause water to flood the earth so that everything on earth that breathes will die. However I'm going to establish My will [for mankind] with you. You, your sons, and daughters-in-law will go in the ark." . . . Noah did everything God demanded. Noah was a good man in the eyes of God, free of guilt, walking with God.

Noah thus became an heir of
the righteousness which is
given in accordance with
faith.

y faith Abraham, when called by God, obeyed by leaving home with no clear destination, for a land that he was to receive as an inheritance from God.

Abraham's faith and inheritance

Genesis 12:1 The Lord (YHWH) told Abram, "Leave your land, your relatives, and your father . . . and go to a place that I'll show you."

Genesis 15:18 The Lord (YHWH) made His will for Abram then, telling him, "I have given this land to your descendants: from the Egyptian river [Nile] to the big river Euphrates, [that is] the [land of the] Kenite[s], the Kenizzite[s], the Kadmonite[s], the Hittite[s], the Perizzite[s], the Rephaim[s], the Amorite[s], the Canaanite[s], the Girgashite[s], and the Jebusite[s]."

Genesis 17:8 [The Lord said,] "I will give you and your descendants the land through which you've traveled, all of Canaan, forever. . . ."

By faith he lived as an alien, a foreigner in the land promised to him, living in his tents with Isaac [his son] and Jacob [his grandson], fellow inheritors of the same promise.

Abraham, the foreigner

Genesis 13:12,18 Abram settled in *Canaan* . . . .Abram moved his tent . . . [to] the oaks of Mamre in *Hebron.*

Genesis 20:1 Abraham traveled toward the *Negev* and [put up his tents] between Kadesh and Shur, then took a trip into *Gevar.*

Genesis 21:34 Abraham traveled through the land of the *Philistines* for a number of days.

Genesis 23:4 [Abraham said,] "I am a stranger, traveling through *Hebron.* [Please] give me a burial place so that I can bury my dead [wife]. . . ."

Genesis 24:62,67 Isaac . . . was staying in the *Negev.* . . . Isaac brought Rebekah into his mother Sarah's tent; he married her and was [thus] comforted after the death of his mother.

Abraham with his son and grandson

[Note: there is no specific scriptural reference to Abram living in the tents with Jacob, his grandson. However the timing of births referenced below supports the Hebrews author's assertion in Hebrews 11:9.]

Genesis 21:5 Abraham was one hundred years old when Isaac, his son, was born.

Genesis 25:26 . . . Isaac was sixty years old when the twins were born to (Rebekah)–[that is Jacob and Esau].

Genesis 25:7 Abraham (lived) one hundred and seventy five years.

[Note: Jacob would have been fifteen years old when Abraham died.]

He was, of course, looking for the city Whose builder and architect is God.

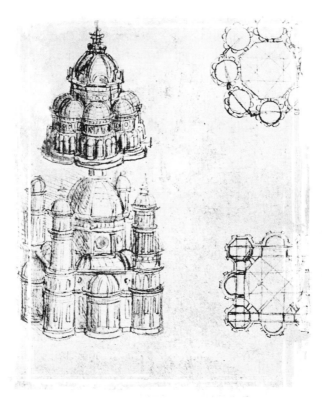

By faith even Sarah herself received the ability to conceive a child, though she was way beyond the proper time of life,

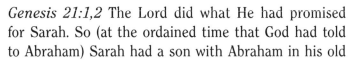

Genesis 21:1,2 The Lord did what He had promised for Sarah. So (at the ordained time that God had told to Abraham) Sarah had a son with Abraham in his old age.

because she considered God,
the One Who had given this
promise, faithful.

 ut of that there was born, then, of one old man (close to death with regard to sexual matters) as many descendants as the stars

Genesis 15:5 (The Word of God came to Abraham saying:) "Do you see the stars in heaven? Count them, if you can. Your descendants (seed) will be as numerous."

Genesis 22:16-18 The Lord (YHWH) declares: "By Myself I have sworn, because you have done this [faithful] thing and not withheld your son, your only son. . . . Indeed, I will bless you greatly and I will multiply your seed like the stars in heaven and like the sand on the shore; moreover, your seed shall possess the entrance to the land of His enemies. In your seed all the countries of the earth shall be blessed because you were obedient to My Voice."

of heaven in number and
innumerable as the sand by
the shore.

All of these people died in faith, having confessed that they themselves were aliens and exiles on earth.

Genesis 23:4 [Abraham said,] "I am a stranger, traveling through. . . ."

Leviticus 25:2,23 <u>God speaks to Moses</u> "(Moses), tell the sons of Israel [this]: 'When you come into the land that I give you, . . . you [better not] ever sell it, because it's Mine. You are nothing but aliens, travelers with Me.'"

Though they welcomed it
from a distance, they died
without receiving the
promised inheritance.

Those who say things like that make it clear they have another country of their own they're looking forward to.

In fact, if the country they were looking for was where they had just been, they had plenty of time to go back.

But they desire a better, heavenly country. So God's not ashamed to be called their God and He's prepared a city for them.

Heavenly country

II Timothy 4:18 The Lord . . . will rescue me [so I can be in] His heavenly kingdom.

I Corinthians 15:50 . . . We can't inherit God's kingdom as humans. Why would anything that dies inherit anything that lasts forever?

I Corinthians 6:9 "Don't you know that the ungodly will not inherit God's kingdom?"

God calls Himself their God

Genesis 26:24 ". . . I am the God of Abraham, your father. . . ."

By faith Abraham, when tested, offered up Isaac; this was the very one who had been given the promises of inheritance from God and yet was ready to offer up his only son.

Genesis 22:2,9-12 "Take your son, your only son, Isaac, whom you love and go right now to the country of Moriah and offer him up to Me as a burnt offering on one of the mountains of which I'll tell you." They came to the place that God had told him about, and Abraham built the altar and arranged the wood and bound his son Isaac and laid him on the altar over the wood. Then Abraham stretched out his hand with the knife to kill his son. But the angel of the Lord (YHWH) called to him from heaven, saying "Abraham, Abraham!", who answered, "Here I am." Then He said to Abraham, "Do not take the lad's life. Do nothing to him, for now I know that you have reverence for God since you have not withheld your only son from Me."

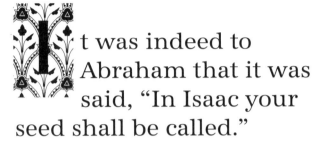

It was indeed to Abraham that it was said, "In Isaac your seed shall be called."

Genesis 21:12 But God said to Abraham, "Don't be stressed over the boy and your maid; listen to what Sarah says because your descendants shall be named after Isaac." [Note: God later gave Isaac's son, Jacob, an alternative name, *Israel*, by which the descendants were called, thus fulfilling God's command.]

Abraham figured that God can raise men from the dead, and he did receive Isaac back from the dead, figuratively speaking.

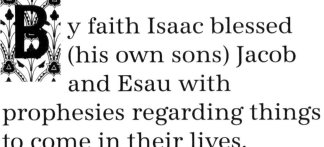 y faith Isaac blessed (his own sons) Jacob and Esau with prophesies regarding things to come in their lives.

Genesis 27:27-30;35,37,39,40 . . . (And Isaac said to Jacob,) "May the Lord (YHWH) bless you with the abundant yield of the earth and may the [Gentile] nations subject themselves to you. Be the head of your brothers and they shall serve you. [May the ones who] curse you, be cursed [instead] and the ones who bless you be blessed [as well]." When Jacob left Isaac, then Esau came in . . . [when Isaac realized Jacob had deceived him by making believe he was the *older* twin, Esau,] he said, "Jacob tricked me and took the blessing that was meant for you." . . . I have just made (Jacob) your master, in fact all [your] relatives will serve him. And I gave him the abundant produce of the earth. What am I supposed to do for you now, (Esau)?" (As Esau cried), Isaac said to him, "You will not live on fertile ground. You'll live by the sword and will serve your brother. But you will break from this burdensome relationship when you become impatient."

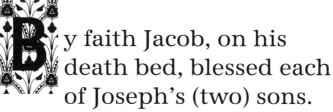

y faith Jacob, on his death bed, blessed each of Joseph's (two) sons. And bowing over his staff, Jacob worshiped God.

Genesis 48:13,14,17,19 Joseph brought both Ephraim and Manasseh close to Israel (his father Jacob). Israel put his right hand on the head of the younger Ephraim, crossing his hands, with the left one on Manasseh's head. . . . This upset Joseph to see Israel's right hand on Ephraim's head [rather than the eldest, Manasseh's]. . . . "I know, I know my son. (Manasseh) will also become a great people, but Ephraim shall be larger and his descendants will become a great many different nations."

By faith Joseph, when he was dying, prophesied the exodus of the sons of Israel, and so gave orders on the burial of his bones.

Genesis 50:24,25 Joseph [one hundred and ten years old–vs 22] told his brothers, "I'm going to die soon. [Don't worry,] God will take care of you and will take you from (Egypt) to the land that He swore He would give to Abraham, Isaac, and Jacob. . . . Now be sure to take my bones there when you go. Swear it!"

By his parents' faith, Moses was hidden when he was born, because he was a beautiful baby and they weren't totally afraid of the king's edict.

Exodus 1:22; 2:1-3 The Pharaoh made an edict that said: "Every (Hebrew) boy that's born shall be thrown into the Nile [to drown], but every girl shall be kept alive." . . . A man and woman (both from the household of Levi) had a new baby boy. (The woman) thought he was beautiful, so she hid him [successfully] for three months. But [finally] . . . she put him in a wicker basket [sealed] with boiled tar and set it in the reeds on the Nile's banks.

By faith Moses, as a grown-up, refused to be called the son of Pharaoh's daughter,

Exodus 2:11 When Moses had grown up, he went out to look at the Hebrews at hard labor [for the Pharaoh]. He saw an Egyptian beating one of the Hebrews. The Hebrews were his blood relatives [so he was furious] and, when he determined no one was looking, he killed the Egyptian and hid him under the sand.

choosing to put up with the poor treatment given the people of God (in Egypt), rather than to enjoy the passing pleasures that sin gives.

By faith he left Egypt, fearless of the Pharaoh's anger, and he endured, even seeing God, Who is never seen.

Exodus 2:15 When the Pharaoh learned what Moses had done, he set out to have Moses killed. But Moses left and settled in Midian. . . .

Exodus 3:4,5 When the Lord (YHWH) saw Moses turn to look [at the angel of the Lord that appeared as a roaring fire in–vs 2] the [middle of a] bush, He called out, "Moses, here I am! . . . Don't come too close. You're standing on ground set apart for God's [use]."

By faith he kept the Passover and sprinkling of blood so that the destroyer of all the firstborn in Egypt would not touch them.

Exodus 12:1-13 The Lord (YHWH) commanded Moses and Aaron (his brother) while they were in Egypt: "Talk to all of Israel and tell them 'on the tenth day of this month (which shall [from now on] be the first month of the year) they shall take one lamb for each household. . . . (It shall be an unblemished one-year-old male . . . sheep or goat.) They shall keep it until the fourteenth day of the month when they shall kill it at twilight. Everyone together [shall kill theirs at twilight]. Then they shall take some of the blood and put it on the [door frame] of the house where they eat the lamb. That lamb needs to be roasted and eaten the same night [it's killed]. Serve it with unleavened bread and bitter herbs. . . . Eat it fast and be ready to go. What's left of it, burn in the fire. That night I am going to kill every firstborn in Egypt—man and beast. . . . I am the Lord (YHWH). . . . When I see the blood (on your door frame), I'll pass over you . . . when I kill the Egyptians. . . .'"

Exodus 12:26,27 (Moses told the people,) "When your children ask you what this rite means, tell them, 'It is a sacrifice to the Lord (YHWH) called *Passover*. [It's to remind us when] the Lord passed over the homes of the sons of Israel in Egypt while He killed the Egyptian [firstborn]." . . .

By faith they passed through the Red Sea as if they were walking across dry land, yet when the Egyptians attempted the same, they drowned.

Exodus 14:21,22,27,28 Moses stretched his arm out over the sea, so the Lord (YHWH) made a strong easterly wind blow all night that divided the waters of the sea to reveal dry land. The sons of Israel went into the sea, walking on the dry land with walls of water to their left and right. . . . (Then) Moses stretched his arm out over the sea [again] and by daybreak the sea had returned to normal. The retreating Egyptians were right in the middle of it, and the Lord (YHWH) overturned their chariots. . . . Not one (of Pharaoh's army that had chased them) made it back alive.

 y faith, the walls of Jericho fell after being surrounded for seven days.

Joshua 5:13-15 When Joshua was at Jericho he looked up to see a man with his sword drawn. . . . (The man said,) "I am captain of the Lord (YHWH)'s angels." Joshua fell on his face and bowed (in servitude) and asked, "What shall I do as [God's] servant?" The captain of angels answered, "Remove your shoes. This land is set apart for God." So that's what Joshua did.

Joshua 6:11-16;20 On Joshua's order, the ark of the testament that was the Lord (YHWH)'s was marched around Jericho one time, then (the men) returned to camp to spend the night. Joshua got up early the next morning [with the] priests, who took the ark. First there were armed men. Then the seven priests went in front of the ark, blowing ram-horn trumpets continuously. A rear guard followed after the ark and everyone marched around the city one time that day. They did this for six days.

The seventh day, after rising at dawn, they marched around the city the same as before. Only [this seventh day] they marched around it seven times. On the seventh time, when the priests blew the ram-horns, Joshua said to the (army) "Shout! The Lord (YHWH) has given you Jericho." . . . So when the priests blew their horns, everyone shouted. It was loud! The wall of the city fell down where it stood [and] every man went straight ahead and captured [Jericho].

By faith Rahab, the Harlot, welcomed the spies in peace, so she didn't die along with the rest of the disobedient.

Joshua 6:23-25 The two young spies went in to Jericho to find Rahab and brought her father and mother and brothers and all her relatives and everything she [owned] and put them [safely] outside Israel's camp. Then they burned the city. . . . But Rahab, the prostitute, and her [entire] father's household and everything she [owned] was safe and she has lived up to this time with the sons of Israel. That's all because she hid the messengers sent by Joshua to spy on Jericho.

W hat more can I say? We don't have time for the like-stories of Gideon, Barak, Samson, Jephthah, David, Samuel, and the prophets.

They conquered kingdoms by faith, performed godly acts, obtained promises, shut the mouths of lions, quenched the power of fire,

escaped the edge of the
sword, were made strong out
of their weaknesses, became
mighty in war, and put
armies to flight.

Women received back their dead by resurrection, others were tortured rather than be released so they would be given a better resurrection.

Resurrected dead

John 11:21-27, 43,44 "If You had been here, Lord, my brother would never have died," Martha said to Jesus. "God will give You whatever You ask Him for, even now," she said. Jesus answered, "Your brother, (Lazarus) will be resurrected." "I know he'll be resurrected in the last [epoch] day," she replied. Jesus then said, "I am the resurrection and the life [as spoken in prophecy]; even those who die shall live if they put faith in Me, and all those who live (having faith in Me) shall never see death." Martha told (Jesus), "Lord I have [always] believed that You are God's Son, the Christ Who is to come to [save] the world." . . . [So] (Jesus) called out loudly, "Lazarus, come on out!" Lazarus came out bound head to toe with cloth wrappings, [alive]! . . .

Torture

Acts 12:1 Herod seized some of the church members so he could [torture] them.

Luke 7:28; 9:9 <u>Jesus speaking</u> "Among human beings, there is no greater person than John (the Baptist). And yet [as great as he is] all those in the kingdom of heaven are greater still." . . . Herod heard about Jesus and said, "I, myself, had John's head cut off, so who (in the world) is *this* man?!"

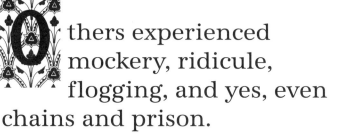

thers experienced mockery, ridicule, flogging, and yes, even chains and prison.

Hebrews 13:23 . . . Timothy, our brother in Christ, has been released [from prison]. . . .

II Timothy 2:3 <u>Paul's letter to Timothy</u> Suffer these difficult, painful conditions with me, as a good soldier [fighting] for Christ.

Ephesians 3:1 You Gentiles, I, Paul, [am] Christ Jesus's prisoner for your sake.

I Corinthians 4:9,10 We apostles, I think, have been put up by God to be a spectacle to the angels and men of this world. We are condemned to death, but we are fools for Christ's sake. . . .

Acts 12:3,4 . . . (Herod) arrested Peter . . . during the Feast of Unleavened Bread and put him in prison. He put [sixteen] soldiers there to guard him until after the Passover, when he intended to bring him before [the Jews].

They were stoned, sawn in two, tempted, put to death with the sword; they went about in sheepskins, goatskins, destitute, afflicted, poorly treated,

Acts 14:19 The Jews came from Antioch and Iconium, and convinced the crowd gathered there to stone Paul. They dragged him out of the city and left him for dead.

Acts 7:55-60; 8:2 (Stephen) filled with God's Holy Spirit, saw into heaven and witnessed God's glory and Jesus standing there at God's right hand. . . . The crowd cried out loud [in unison] and, covering their ears, they rushed forward as one. [Stephen was driven out of the city], then they stoned him. "Lord Jesus," he called, "take my spirit. Don't hold this against them, Lord!" Then (Stephen)'s spirit rested. . . . Starting that day, the church (of believers) in Jerusalem was persecuted heavily and, except for the apostles, was scattered throughout the areas of Judea and Samaria.

Acts 12:2 James [one of the disciples], John's brother, was actually killed by a sword.

Matthew 3:4 John [the Baptist] wore clothing made of camel hair with a leather belt around his waist. . . .

Wandering around in deserts and mountains and caves and holes in the ground. (The world wasn't worthy of these men).

All of them gained approval through their faith, but did not [yet] receive the inheritance that was promised to them.

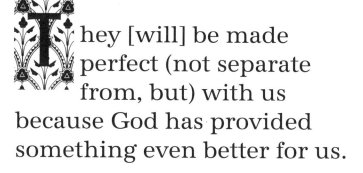 hey [will] be made perfect (not separate from, but) with us because God has provided something even better for us.

James 1,2,3 [Dear] siblings in Christ, be happy when you are tested, since the very testing of your faith produces endurance.

I Peter 4:13 Be happy as long as you're suffering [on behalf] of Christ, so that when He's revealed in His glory, you can be absolutely jubilant.

John 3:36 The one who has faith in the Son shall live forever, but the one who *does not obey* the Son shall not live, and instead incur God's lasting wrath.

Isaiah 45:4-7 For Israel's sake, My servant, My chosen one, I also called you, personally. I gave you a title with honor [*Christian*], even though you have not known Me [as Israel did]. [Let Me introduce Myself:] I am the Lord (YHWH), the only One. There is no other God but Me. I will [protect] you, although you have not known Me. By My doing these things, they may understand from east to west that there is no one like Me. I am the Lord (YHWH), the only One. The One Who created light and darkness, Who is the force behind peace and disaster. I am the Lord (YHWH) Who causes all these things [to be].

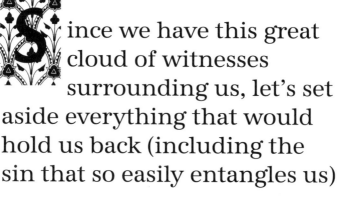

Since we have this great cloud of witnesses surrounding us, let's set aside everything that would hold us back (including the sin that so easily entangles us)

<u>Abandoning all obstacles to finishing the race</u>

Romans 13:12 [The age of] darkness [and sin] is almost finished; the dawn of God's reign is at hand. Let's abandon our secret [commitment to] sin and defend ourselves [against it] with the light [of Christ].

I Peter 2:1 Abandon meanness and lies, and pretenses [of piety] and jealousies and false statements defaming another's reputation.

Ephesians 4:22-24 Lusts [are] born of deceit; [Satan lies to you about the benefits, however temporary they may be], [and so lusts] corrupt. Give up this old [dishonest] self, [then,] and refresh your attitude. Represent God as His new creation in perfect goodness and truth.

I Corinthians 9:24 Only one person wins the prize in a race, though many compete. Run to win.

and let's run with endurance
the race that we're challenged
with today.

e must] fix our eyes on (the goal), which is Jesus. Jesus wrote the book on faith and was a perfectionist in that regard. (He) endured the cross for the

The goal

Philippians 3:14 I keep moving toward the goal because I want God to call me up to [join] Christ, Jesus [to resurrect me from the dead—vs 11].

Philippians 3:8 . . . I've lost everything, but [as far as I'm concerned] it was all garbage [anyway]—things I trashed in order to gain Christ.

Ephesians 1:18 [I pray] that the Father of our Lord Jesus Christ, the God of glory, will give you wisdom and reveal Himself to you that you may know Him and know His truth.

joy ahead, though (He) despised the shame, and (He) sat down [in the seat of highest honor] to the right of God's throne.

Jesus's faith

Hebrews 1:3 Jesus is the exact representation of God's nature and holds all things together by the power of His Word. He made purification of sins. He sat down at God's right.

Philippians 2:8 In His appearance as a man, He humbled Himself *by becoming obedient to God* to the point of death, death on a cross, yet.

Hebrews 2:9 By God's grace to us, Christ was made, for a little while, lower than "Elohim" [God's angels] so He could experience death for everyone. Christ was crowned with glory and honor because of the suffering of death.

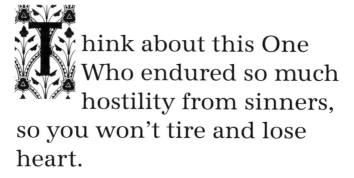 hink about this One Who endured so much hostility from sinners, so you won't tire and lose heart.

Galatians 6:9 Let's not lose heart. Let's continue to do good things and not grow tired from suffering. Because we shall reap [what we sow—vs 7].

James 5:13-15 Are any of [you] suffering? Allow [yourself] to pray. . . . Are any of you sick? Allow the elders of the church to pray over [you] and anoint [you] with oil in [Christ's] name. For the prayer given with faith [that God will grant it—Mark 11:24] will make [you] well. And the Lord will resurrect [you] and forgive any sins that [you] have committed.

Hebrews 2:10 In bringing many sons to glory, it was fitting for Christ to perfect Himself as man's Saviour through suffering, as all things are made for Christ and made through Christ.

Matthew 10:22 <u>Jesus speaking to the disciples</u>
"Everyone will hate you because I am called *the Christ*,
but it's the one who endures to the end who'll be
saved."

Matthew 24:13 But the person shall be saved who
endures [through it all] to the end.

Hebrews 10:36 You need to endure, so that when you've
done God's will, you may receive that (inheritance) He
promised you.

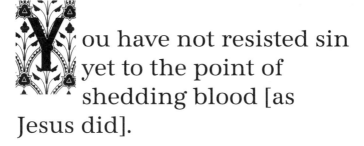

You have not resisted sin yet to the point of shedding blood [as Jesus did].

Galatians 2:20 <u>Paul to the churches of Galatia</u> I was crucified with Christ so my old self is no longer alive. Christ's [spirit] lives in me. My new life in this body is based on faith in the Son of God, who loved me and made Himself an offering to God [to wipe out my sins].

Revelation 2:3 <u>What the Lord God told John to write to the church in Ephesus</u> '. . . You have perseverance and, because of My name, you have endured and have not grown tired with suffering.'

And don't forget God's clear warning to you as sons of God: "My son, do not lightly regard the discipline of the Lord nor faint when He reprimands you,

Proverbs 3:11,12 "Don't reject the Lord (YHWH)'s discipline or hate His reprimand. He reprimands the ones He loves, as a father does a son. . . ."

Revelation 3:19 <u>What the Lord told John to write to the churches in Laodicea</u> 'The ones whom I love, I reprimand and discipline. So be devoted [to Me] and turn away from sin.'

Psalm 119:75 I realize Your judgments are perfect and good; as a faithful [teacher and father], You strike me.

for those who the Lord loves,
He disciplines and He whips
every son whom He receives."

It is, in fact, discipline that you endure. God is clearly with you as with sons. (For what son is there who is not disciplined by his father?)

Deuteronomy 3:5 <u>Moses speaking to the sons of Israel regarding their forty years in the wilderness</u> "Know in your heart that the Lord (YHWH) your God was disciplining you as a [father] disciplines his son."

Proverbs 19:18 While there's still hope for his reformation, discipline your son, that is unless you wish to be the cause of his death.

Proverbs 23:13 A child is not going to die from being beaten with a rod; don't hold back when you discipline a child.

Proverbs 13:24 The one who spares his son from the rod hates him. If he loved him, he would discipline his son constantly.

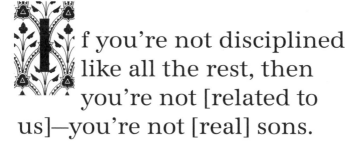 f you're not disciplined like all the rest, then you're not [related to us]—you're not [real] sons.

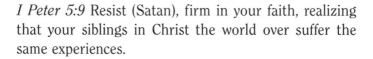

I Peter 5:9 Resist (Satan), firm in your faith, realizing that your siblings in Christ the world over suffer the same experiences.

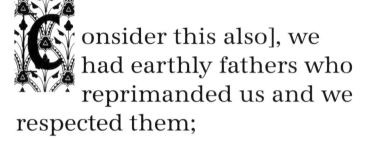 onsider this also], we had earthly fathers who reprimanded us and we respected them;

Numbers 16:22 [Moses and Aaron] fell upon their faces [to God]: "O God of the spirits of all man and beast and bird, are you going to condemn everyone over the sin of man?"

shouldn't we want to be
subjected to the discipline of
the Father of our spirit and
thereby live?

For (our fathers) reprimanded us a little, whatever seemed best; but God disciplines us for our own good so we'll share in His holiness.

Revelation 2:26 'To the one who overcomes and acts as I did to the end, I will give authority over the [Gentile] nations. And that one shall shepherd them with a rod of iron . . . *just as I was given* authority to do so from *My* Father. I will give him the morning star. [Compare Revelation 22:6 I, Jesus, . . . am . . . the bright morning star.]

II Peter 1:14 He granted us His priceless inheritance so that as beneficiaries of the [eternal] life and godliness we could share in the divine state of being— all that after we [are rescued] from the dishonesty of the world born out of the intense cravings [of man].

All discipline when it's given seems a sad affair, yet to those who've been trained by it, (they know) it gives way to peaceful godliness.

Psalm 73:21-24 I wasn't thinking, was ignorant like an animal, [and] I was bitter, pierced to the core. But I am [sticking] with You, Lord. You've taken me by the hand and will guide me with Your advice. Then [You'll] welcome me to glory.

Psalm 119:165 Nothing causes those to stumble who love Your law [O, Lord]; they have [Your] great peace.

Psalm 85:8-10 . . . (God) will speak [about] peace to His godly people [and] not let them fall back into immorality. His salvation is [close] to those who revere Him, [His] glory will stay in our land. Kindness from love and faithfulness have come together. Pure goodness and perfection and peace have each [blessed] the other.

Isaiah 32:17,18 Perfection and goodness make for peace and quiet and security.

James 3:17 Wisdom [that comes] from heaven is first and foremost pure. It is also peaceful, gentle, flexible, forgiving, productive, stable, and true to itself.

 o after all that, strengthen your weak hands and feeble knees,

Isaiah 35:3,4 Encourage those with weak hands and wobbling knees. Tell those who are [scared to death], "Don't be afraid, take courage. Look now, your God is going to come with a vengeance. He will repay. But He's going to save *you*.

Luke 21:19,18 <u>Jesus speaking</u> "You will win your own soul by your perseverance, but not one hair of your head will die."

James 5:8 Be patient, be strong-hearted, because the Lord is coming soon.

Psalm 73:26 My body and heart may fail, but God is [solid as] a rock and all that I'll ever need for body and soul.

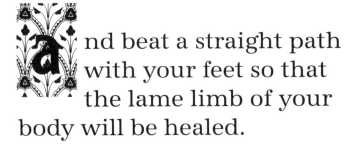 nd beat a straight path with your feet so that the lame limb of your body will be healed.

Proverbs 4:26 Watch where you're going and your path of progress will be made secure [by God].

Romans 2:7 (God will reward) everlasting life to the ones who persevere and do good things because they want honor and glory and immortality. Confess your sins to each other, pray for each other so that [God] may heal you. (A righteous man's prayers can accomplish a lot.)

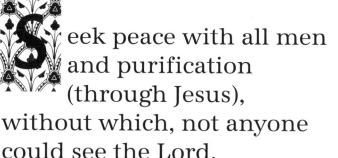 eek peace with all men and purification (through Jesus), without which, not anyone could see the Lord.

Psalm 24:3-5 Who will be allowed to come up to God's [Mountain of Zion]? Who will be permitted to stand in the holy place [in His tabernacle]? [The answer is this:] the one who is innocent in action and intent, who hasn't given his soul over to lies or sworn with clever mis-statements. This one shall be blessed with perfection and goodness from the God Who saved him.

Revelation 22:4 [His bond-servants] shall serve Him. And *they will look on His face,* His name [always on their mind] emblazoned on their foreheads.

I John 3:2 . . . We do know that, when Christ appears, we shall be like Him, because we shall see Him in His true state.

Matthew 5:9,8 The peacemakers are blessed, as they will be called sons of God. The pure-hearted are blessed, as they will see God.

Romans 14:19 Let's go for things that make for peace. Let's give each other positive reinforcement.

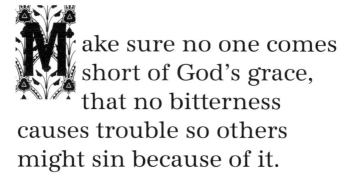 ake sure no one comes
short of God's grace,
that no bitterness
causes trouble so others
might sin because of it.

Hebrews 4:1 Even though a promise remains of entering God's tranquil rest—not death—let's be prudent so no one misses out on it.

Galatians 5:7 You were running (the race) well—who got in your way of obeying the truth, [or the Word of God—John 17:17]?

II Corinthians 6:1 I beg you, don't [waste God's forgiveness by] thinking [time] doesn't matter . . . (because) . . . today is "the day of salvation".

Make sure also that there is no immoral or godless person (among you) like Esau, who shed his birthright for one measly meal.

II Corinthians 6:14 Don't be tied in a burdensome union with those who don't believe in (the gospel), [resurrection and the kingdom of God and Christ Jesus]. What do [you really] have in common with lawlessness [since you have the promise of] perfection and goodness? Whereas you walk in the light [that illuminates the knowledge of God], they are in the dark [blinded to the truth]. What kind of partnership is that?

I Timothy 1:13 <u>Paul writing to Timothy</u> . . . I used to say sacrilegious things; I persecuted (Christians) and was violently aggressive. After all that, (God) showed me forgiveness because I was ignorant in my unbelief— [I just didn't know].

Genesis 25:28-34 Isaac loved [his eldest twin] Esau because Esau enjoyed [the hunt]. Rebekah, however, loved Jacob. Esau came in from the field [one day] and asked Jacob to give him some stew that Jacob had cooked. "I'm starved," he said. "Please give me some of your red concoction." . . . "First sell me the rights you received at birth [being the eldest]," replied Jacob. Esau retorted, "[What of it?] My birthright is useless to me dead. And I'm about to die of starvation anyway if you don't give me some of that." [Jacob was persistent though; it was no joke to him]. "No, swear to me now— [your birthright for this stew]," he said. So Esau swore and Jacob gave him some lentil stew. Esau ate, drank, and excused himself. Thus Esau sold his birthright to Jacob, as if it were worthless.

As you know, afterwards, when he tried to inherit the blessing, he was rejected and he found no forgiveness, though he sought it with fear.

Genesis 27:35,37,39 [When Isaac realized Jacob had deceived him by making believe he was the *older* twin, Esau,] he said, "Jacob tricked me and took the blessing that was meant for you. . . . I have just made (Jacob) your master, in fact all [your] relatives will serve him. And I gave him the abundant produce of the earth. What am I supposed to do for you now, (Esau)?" . . . (As Esau cried), Isaac said to him, "You will not live on fertile ground. You'll live by the sword and will serve your brother."

ow (unlike Moses) you have not come to a mountain that can be touched, and to a blazing fire and to darkness and gloominess and a tornado,

Deuteronomy 4:11,12 <u>Moses reminding all of Israel</u>
"You came to the base of the mountain, which burned with fire to the center of heaven, surrounded by blackness and clouds and gloom. Then you heard the Lord (YHWH)'s voice from the middle of the fire, though you saw no one."

nd to a trumpet blast and words that sounded so [awesome] that those who heard them begged that the speaker stop.

Exodus 19:16,19 On the morning of the third day, there were thunderous sounds and flashes of lightning and a thick cloud on the mountain top. There was a loud trumpet-like noise and everyone in the camp was trembling. . . . When the sound grew increasingly louder, Moses called [to God], who answered him with thunder.

Exodus 20:18,19 When (the sons of Israel) realized [that] the noise and lightning and trumpet sound and smoking mountain [were communications from God], they trembled [with fear] and stood off a ways. They told Moses, "We'll listen to *you* but please don't let God speak to us, or we might die."

They couldn't bear the command: "If even one animal touches the mountain, it will be stoned."

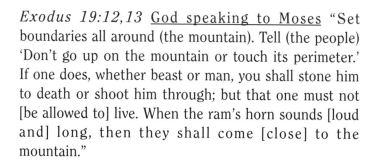

Exodus 19:12,13 <u>God speaking to Moses</u> "Set boundaries all around (the mountain). Tell (the people) 'Don't go up on the mountain or touch its perimeter.' If one does, whether beast or man, you shall stone him to death or shoot him through; but that one must not [be allowed to] live. When the ram's horn sounds [loud and] long, then they shall come [close] to the mountain."

So frightening was the whole sight that even Moses said, "I am trembling; I'm scared to death."

Deuteronomy 9:19 (These are Moses's words to all of Israel—vs 1) "I was afraid of God's fiery anger toward you; He was going to destroy you. . . ."

ather, you have come to Mount Zion, the city of the living God, the heavenly Jerusalem and to a massive assembly of angels.

Psalm 48:1 The Lord (YHWH) is great; He will be greatly praised in His holy mountain, the *city of our God.*

Philippians 3:20 We are citizens of heaven, whereby we also eagerly wait for our Saviour, the Lord Jesus Christ.

Hebrews 11:10 (Abraham) . . . was of course looking for the city Whose builder and architect is God.

Revelation 21:1-3 I saw a new heaven and earth. The first heaven and the first earth died. There wasn't any sea at all [in the new earth]. I saw the city set apart as God's *new Jerusalem.* And it was coming from Him down out of the heavens, made beautiful like a bride for her husband. A loud voice from heaven said, "Look now, God's house is among mankind and He shall live with man and they shall be His people; God Himself shall be in the middle of them[!]"

Psalm 2:6 "But as for Me, I have installed My King upon Zion, the nation I set apart for Myself."

Revelation 14:1 I looked and there I saw the Lamb standing on Mount Zion. With Him there were one hundred and forty thousand that had His name and His Father's name written on their foreheads.

Revelation 5:11 I looked and around the throne and the living creatures and the elders there were thousands upon thousands of angels with (loud) voices.

Daniel 7:10 A flowing river of fire was coming out in front of Him; thousands upon thousands *were attending Him*, and myriads upon myriads were standing in front of Him. The court sat, then the books were opened.

Isaiah 2:2-4 <u>Isaiah, the prophet, saw the *Word* in a vision</u> In the last [epoch] the [nation] wherein the Lord (YHWH) lives will be founded on the [nation] which is the leader of all [countries]. It will be raised above the lesser [countries]. [People from] all nations will go there in streams. Many will come, saying "Let's go to God's country, to where the God of Israel lives, so we can gain knowledge of God and walk in His paths [He prepared for us"–Proverbs 4:36].

The law will be issued from Zion, the Word of the Lord (YHWH) from Jerusalem. He will judge and decide for the nations. [For their part] the peoples will re-make their swords into plow blades. And they'll re-make their spears into pruning devices. The nations will be marked by peace and never learn war-making again. [Note: the plow and pruning devices referenced in this verse are traditionally perceived as a representation of peacetime endeavors. However, they may be equally symbolic representations of God's harvest of the earth

(the plow blades) and His pruning away of those who have no part in Christ, the vine. Since the result of pruning is that new growth is encouraged on the plant, we could take this to mean that the body of believers (the branches) as an outgrowth of Christ will increase. We must then also consider: if "the people" are the ones turning their implements of war into tools for God's harvest, will God be employing these same people to carry through His harvest of the earth?]

You've come) to the general assembly and church of the firstborn recorded [in the Book of Life] in heaven, and to God, the judge of all,

To the general assembly and church of the firstborn Israel, the *firstborn* son

Exodus 4:22 The Lord (YHWH) speaking to Moses "Tell Pharaoh, 'The Lord says this, "Israel is My firstborn son."'"

Jeremiah 31:9 Jeremiah, the prophet, telling what the Lord said "They shall return weeping; I shall show them the way through their prayers. I will make them walk by streams along a straight road; they shall not trip and fall. For (you know) I am a father to Israel, and Ephraim (Joseph's son, Jacob's grandson) is My firstborn.

[Note: Joseph's son, Ephraim, was part of the first generation of Israel (Jacob) to be born in Egypt.]

Hosea 11:1 When Israel was young, I loved him; thus I called My son out of Egypt.

and to the spirits of godly men perfected [by Christ's sacrifice].

Christ as firstborn

Psalm 2:7,8 David prophesying about the Christ, Who is speaking "(God) said to Me, 'You are My Son, today I have begotten You. . . . I will absolutely give the nations as Your inheritance, and the very ends of the earth as Your possession.'"

Believers as first-fruit of the Christ's inheritance

James 1:18 (The Father) brought us [forward] through the Word [Jesus Christ] of truth, so that we could be a certain first-fruit from all the creatures that He created. This is what He desired [for us].

Revelation 14:4 . . . (The virgins) have been redeemed from mankind as first-fruits to God and the Lamb.

To God the Judge

Psalm 50:6,4 The [angels in the] heavens proclaim that He is perfect and good. God Himself is [the] judge. . . . He calls everyone [together] in heaven and on earth in order to judge His people.

Psalm 94:2 O Judge of the earth, arise and repay the proud-hearted.

To the spirits of godly men

Revelation 6:9,11 <u>John, the disciple and apostle's vision</u> When He broke the fifth seal, I saw the souls of the martyrs underneath the altar. These were martyrs for (Jesus Christ) the Word of God—they stuck to their account of the truth until they were killed. Each of them was given a white robe and told that they should rest a little longer, for the number of their fellow servants who were to be killed as they they had been was not yet complete.

Revelation 20:4 I saw (the twenty-four elders) [who sat down] on their thrones, having been given the authority to judge. And there were the souls of the people who had been beheaded because they were telling about Jesus, the Word of God. There were also the souls of the people who did not [accept] the mark of the beast on their hand or forehead and of the ones who had not worshiped the beast. These all came to life and had supreme power with Christ for [an epoch of] a thousand years. . . .

Perfected

Hebrews 11:40 They [will] be made perfect (not separate from, but) with us because God has provided something even better for us.

And [finally] (you've come) to Jesus, the mediator of the new Will and Testament, and to His sprinkled blood which speaks [more powerfully] than the blood of Abel [did].

To Jesus

Revelation 21:7 Christ speaking on His throne "The one who overcomes shall inherit these things. *I will be his God and he will be My son.*"

Jesus, the mediator

I Timothy 2:5 There is one God, also one mediator between God and mankind, the man Christ Jesus.

Jesus's sprinkled blood

I Peter 1:2 May forgiveness, mercy, and peace be yours in the fullest by the purifying work of the Spirit, according to God the Father's plan, so that you may *obey* Jesus Christ and therefore be sprinkled with His blood. [Note: Compare with the atonement, forgiveness, and purification process described in Leviticus 16, pages 124-129.]

Hebrews 10:22 [Jesus Christ's] sprinkled blood [sacrifice] has cleansed our hearts from their evil intentions; [His] purifying water [of life] has made ready our bodies [for God]. [Since our hearts control our thoughts, which control our bodies,] be convicted by your faith, then, so you can approach God where He lives.

Be sure you don't refuse God Who speaks [to you]. Because if those who were warned by the prophets didn't escape, how

Isaiah 1:24-28 The Lord (YHWH), God of the angels, The Mighty One of Israel says this: "I will get rid of those who fight against Me and will take revenge on My enemies. I will also turn My hand on *you* and with burning acid melt away [those who have] bonded with you and made you impure. I will remove your impurities [–Zephaniah 3:11]. After that I will let you have your judges and counselors just like you used to [long ago]. Then you'll be called the city of perfect goodness and purity, a faithful city."

Zion will be purchased back to God with justice, and those who come back [to God], with perfection and goodness. But the ones who abandon the Lord (YHWH) shall meet their doom. All those who [flagrantly] sin against God will be defeated together.

Hebrews 2:2,3 . . . (If) every sin and disobedience has received a fair, equivalent "pay-back", then how shall we escape if we ignore so great a deliverance from sin and its penalties? . . .

much less chance shall we
have to escape God Himself
Who warns [us] from heaven?

During that time [with Moses] the earth trembled from His voice. Yet He has promised: "One more time I will shake not just the earth but the heavens as well."

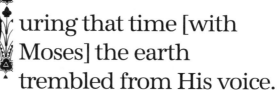

Judges 5:4,5 <u>The song of Deborah</u> "Lord when You went out from Seir, when you marched from the field of Edom, the earth shook; the heavens dripped. The clouds even dripped with water. The mountains flowed at the presence of the Lord (YHWH)—that is Sinai flowed at the presence of the Lord (YHWH), the God of Israel."

Psalm 68:7,8 <u>David's Psalm</u> O God, when you went before Your people, when you marched through the wilderness, the earth shook; the heavens dripped at the presence of God. This is Sinai that shook at the presence of God, the God of Israel.

Exodus 19:18 Mount Sinai was covered in smoke, because the Lord (YHWH) had come down in fire to the mountain. Its smoke was thick and black and went up like the smoke of a furnace. The whole mountain shook violently.

Haggai 2:6 <u>Haggai, the prophet, speaking the words of God</u> "This is what the Lord of angels says: 'One more time (that will be in a while) I will shake the heavens and earth–that includes the sea and the dry land.'"

his phrase, "One more time", suggests the removal (or shaking) of things [man] created, leaving the things which will not shake loose.

I Corinthians 7:31 . . . The earth's structure is dying. . . .

I John 2:17 . . . The inhabited earth is dying as are the cravings [of man]; but the one who follows God's will lives forever. [Compare Hebrews 1:10-12 and corresponding references, pages 34-36.]

Isaiah 34:4 The [angels] of heaven will rot. The sky will be rolled up like a scroll. Its hosts will wither and die, like a leaf falls off of a vine.

Isaiah 54:10 "The mountains and hills may tremble and fall; but, because I love you, I will always show kindness to you. My testament of peace will not shake loose," says the Lord (YHWH). . . .

Therefore, considering that we're receiving a kingdom which (obviously) can't be shaken, [the least we can do is] to offer a service to God that He might find acceptable.

<u>Unshakable kingdom</u>

Isaiah 65:17,18 "Look, I create new heavens and a new earth, and everything that existed in the past will be totally forgotten. Be happy and forever celebrate what I create; I create Jerusalem for celebration and her people for happiness.

Daniel 2:44 <u>Daniel interpreting Nebuchadnezzar's dream</u> . . . God of heaven will establish a kingdom that will exist forever and never be destroyed and never be [occupied by] another people.

Revelation 21:4,5 . . . There shall no longer be any death nor therefore any mourning, nor crying, nor pain. The One Who sits on the throne said, "Look, I am making everything new." . . .

<u>Service</u>

Isaiah 65:13,14 Look now, My servants shall eat. . . .
Look now, My servants shall drink. . . . Look, for My
servants shall celebrate; Look, for My servants shall
shout with glee. . . .

Psalm 31:6 (I am Your servant, Lord). Look down on
me with Your radiant light. Save me out of Your
kindness and love for me.

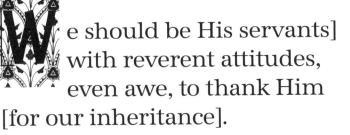

[We should be His servants] with reverent attitudes, even awe, to thank Him [for our inheritance].

Matthew 20:26-28 ". . . Anyone who wishes to achieve greatness among you and anyone who wishes to be your leader shall [first] be your servant, your slave. The Son of Man did not come so [you could] serve Him, but as a servant, Himself, and to pay the ransom price for many lives with His own."

Revelation 5:11-14 John's vision I looked and heard many angels' voices around the throne and there were thousands upon thousands and also the living beings and the elders. They said with a [huge] voice: "The Lamb that was killed is worthy to receive power and riches and wisdom and might, honor, glory, and blessings." And I heard every created thing in heaven and on earth, all things under the earth and in the sea, saying, "May God, who sits on the throne, and the Lamb have all blessing and honor and glory and control for ever and ever." The four living beings said over and over again "Amen." The elders fell down and worshiped.

Revelation 7:11 All the angels were standing around
the throne. . . . Then they fell on their faces before it
and worshiped God. . . .

 est we ever forget,] our God is a consuming fire.

Deuteronomy 4:24 "The Lord (YHWH) your God is a consuming fire. . . ."

Deuteronomy 9:3 "The Lord (YHWH) your God, crossing in front of you, [is] a consuming fire. . . ."

Isaiah 33:14 "Which one of us can live with the consuming fire? . . ."

 ontinue to love your
fellow brothers and
sisters in Christ.

I Thessalonians 4:9 <u>Paul (with Timothy and Silvanus) writing to the church of the Thessalonians</u> You are taught by God Himself so you don't need [me or] anyone [else] to write you about that.

Romans 12:10 <u>Paul writes to the Christians in Rome</u> With the same love you reserve for your family, devote yourself to and honor each other.

<u>Peter writing to the Christians gathered around Pontus, Galatia, Cappadocia, Asia, and Bithynia</u>

I Peter 2:17 Honor all mankind, love your siblings in Christ, respect God, and honor your head of state.

I Peter 1:22 Since you have made your [hearts] pure by [following] the truth, love your siblings in Christ from the heart so that it is a [true] love.

Be sure and show hospitality to strangers, because some have entertained angels this way without knowing who they really were.

Genesis 19:1-3 Lot, rising to meet the two angels who came into Sodom that evening, bowed all the way to the ground. He said, "Please, my lords, stay at my house for the night and bathe, then you can leave early in the morning. . . . (Although they first refused,) Lot insisted, so they went to his house where he prepared a feast for them. . . .

Genesis 18:1-5 The Lord (YHWH) came up (to Abraham) while he was sitting by his tent [cooling himself in the shade] by the oaks of Mamre. When (Abraham) looked up, there were (the Lord and two other men) standing (under the oaks). He ran over to them and bowed all the way to the ground and said, "Please, if you are pleased with me, [Lord], stay here in the shade and let me bring some water to wash your feet. I'll get some bread; [You're probably hungry]. Then you can go on after you've visited with me, your servant." They said, "[That's fine, Abraham,] go ahead."

Matthew 25:40 "[Christ] the King will . . . say . . . 'you [gave] to Me when you [looked after] one of My siblings, even the lowest class one or the least powerful.'"

Think of the prisoners, as if you were there with them, and also those who are treated badly since we all belong to the body (of believers in Christ) (for which they suffer).

Hebrews 10:34 You showed sympathy to the prisoners and accepted the seizure of your property with happiness, knowing you had a better possession, an everlasting one.

Colossians 4:3 <u>Paul writing</u> . . . [Pray] for us . . . [Who] have been imprisoned because we teach about the Word of God, so that we may have an opportunity to speak about the mystery of Christ.

Ephesians 6:19,20 Pray for me so [God] will give me the words when I open my mouth, to be bold in revealing the mysteries of the true account of Christ, even while I'm in chains.

Matthew 25:36,40 . . . You visited Me when I was imprisoned. . . . So, "[Christ] the King will . . . say . . . 'you [gave] to Me when you [looked after] one of My siblings, even the lowest class one or the least powerful.'"

All of you honor marriage, and let the sexual relationship between husband and wife be pure, because God will judge those who have sex out

I Thessalonians 4:3 . . . The will of God . . . is that you abstain from sexual immorality.

I Corinthians 6:18 . . . The (sexually) immoral man actually sins against his own body.

I Corinthians 7:5 (Those of you who are married,) don't deprive each other (of sex) unless it's a specific break for prayer. Even then, come back together so you won't be tempted by Satan to lose self-control.

Galatians 5:21 . . . I am warning you now . . . those who make a practice of the following things won't be able to claim their inheritance in the kingdom of God: immorality, impurity, sensuality, idolatry, witchcraft, hate, warring, jealousy, rage, causing disputes and dissensions and heresies, envy, carousing, and drunkenness.

Exodus 20;14 <u>One of the Ten Commandments</u> "You shall not have sex with someone else's partner."

of lust and those who have sexual relations with someone else's marriage partner.

ree your life from the love
of money and be happy
with what you have; God
Himself said, "I will never
desert you, nor will I turn my
back on you (or sell you out)."

God will never desert you

Joshua 1:5 <u>God speaking to Joshua</u> . . . I will be [there] with you without fail; I won't desert you. . . .

Deuteronomy 31:6,7 <u>Moses speaks to all of Israel first and then to Joshua</u> "Don't be afraid, take courage and be strong. God Himself, the Lord (YHWH), goes with you without fail and will never turn His back on you. . . . You also Joshua, be strong and courageous . . . with the people. You shall [be the one to] lead these people into the land the Lord (YHWH) gave under oath to them as an inheritance.

Colossians 3:5 . . . Greed . . . amounts to the idolizing of another god.

Ephesians 5:3,4 . . . Don't (be greedy,) [instead] give thanks [to God].

I Timothy 3:3 [Do] not [be] addicted to . . . the love of money.

Luke 21:4 <u>Jesus speaking</u> "[Those men] made an offering to God from what they had left over [after spending on themselves], while [this lady] put in everything she had to live on, [even] in her poverty."

We (can) confidently say: "The Lord is my helper, I won't be afraid—what can man do to me?"

—Psalm 118:6

Psalm 118:6 The Lord (YHWH) is for me–I won't be afraid. What can man do to [hurt] me?

Psalm 120:1 I called out to God when I was [in] trouble and He answered me.

Psalm 18:6 I cried to God for help in my distress. From where He stays, He heard my call. . . .

Psalm 86:7 When I am in trouble, I will call on You (Lord), because (I know) You will answer me.

Think about your leaders who spoke God's word to you and imitate their faith, remembering how they died for it.

Hebrews 11:35-38 Women received back their dead by resurrection, others were tortured rather than be released so they would be given a better resurrection. Others experienced mockery, ridicule, flogging, and yes, even chains and prison. They were stoned, sawn in two, tempted, put to death with the sword; they went about in sheepskins, goatskins, destitute, afflicted, poorly treated, wandering around in deserts and mountains and caves and holes in the ground. . . . (The world wasn't worthy of these men).

Hebrews 11:1,2 Faith is when you are sure of things you hope for, though you have seen no evidence. By faith men through the ages gained (God's) approval.

Hebrews 6:12 So that you won't be slow in this, just imitate the faithful and patient people who inherit God's promises.

 esus Christ is the same yesterday, today, and forever!

Hebrews 1:10-12 And (of the Son he also says:) "You, Lord, in the beginning laid the foundation of the earth. You created the heavens with Your own hands. They will both perish, but You will remain. All of them will wear out like a garment; they will be changed like clothing; and You will roll them up as an overcoat. But You are always the same and You will live forever."

Daniel 7:13,14 The Son of Man was presented before the ancient of days [God] and was given glory and rule over a kingdom. All the people of all the countries were to serve Him. His control will last forever. His kingdom won't be destroyed.

Revelation 22:13,14 "I am the Alpha and Omega; the first, the last; the beginning and the end." Those who cleanse themselves are blessed in that they will have the right to the tree of life and to enter the (holy) city [*new Jerusalem*].

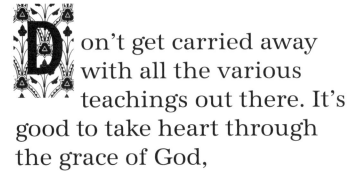**D**on't get carried away with all the various teachings out there. It's good to take heart through the grace of God,

Hebrews 2:1 Pay close attention so that we won't drift away from what we've heard.

Hebrews 3:1 . . . Think about Jesus—He was sent by God to teach and be our high priest.

John 17:8 Jesus praying "The words which You gave Me I have given to them, and they received them and truly did understand that I came forth from You, and they believed that You did indeed send Me."

II John 7-9 . . . Watch yourselves so as not to lose ground, so that you will receive your total reward. Anyone who goes too far out on a limb and doesn't live by the teaching of Christ does not have God with him; on the other hand, the person who lives by the teaching has both the Father and the Son with him.

rather than be occupied with teachings that aren't going to benefit you anyway.

he priests of the tabernacle have no right to eat at our altar.

Hebrews 7:28 The Law, you know, appoints as high priests men, who are naturally weak. But the Word of God's oath, which came after the Law, appoints His Son, made perfect forever.

Hebrews 7:12 The Law necessarily changed when the priesthood changed.

Hebrews 7:15-19 . . . Then the first [order] was set aside because (1) it was weak and useless (and did not make anything perfect after all), and (2) a better hope came about and, through that hope, we come closer to God.

hey take the bodies of the animals whose blood was used as a sin offering in the holy place by their high priest outside the camp to be burned.

Hebrews 9:13,14 If the blood of goats and bulls and the sprinkled ashes of the heifer over the impure, purify the body, since Christ, through the everlasting Holy Spirit, offered Himself perfect to God; will His blood cleanse your conscience from things you did leading to death under the Law, so you may serve the living God?

Hebrews 9:22,23 So according to the Law, almost all things are made clean (purified) with blood, and without death and bloodshed there is no inherited forgiveness. Therefore, it was necessary for our earthly copies of heavenly things to be cleansed with these [types of death and sacrifices]. But the heavenly things themselves [are cleansed] with better sacrifices than these.

Hebrews 9:15 . . . For this reason (His self-sacrifice), He is the mediator of a new contract between God and man [God's new Will and Testament].

Likewise, Jesus was made to suffer outside the gate, so He could purify the people with His own blood.

Hebrews 10:10,14,19,20 By this (second, new order) we have been purified for God through the [sacrificial] offering of the body of Christ, once and for all time. . . . By one offering, He has perfected those who are set apart for purification. . . . Therefore, brothers, we [should] have confidence to enter the holy place by the blood sacrifice of Jesus, by the new and living way initiated for us through the veil of His flesh.

So we need to go outside the camp to where He is, bearing His disgrace and censorship.

Leviticus 16:15,27 "Next he shall slaughter the goat that is the sin offering for the people and bring its blood inside the veil. . . . [Its carcass] shall be taken outside the camp—[the] hide and flesh and refuse shall be burned by the fire. . . ."

Hebrews 8:4-6 According to the Law, Christ would not be a priest at all here on earth, since the Law already defines the Levites to act as priests and offer gifts. But they only symbolize and foreshadow the real heavenly things. . . .

Hebrews 10:1 Since the Law only foreshadows the good inheritance and is not the inheritance itself, it can never be the (legal) instrument to make perfect those who draw near to God by the same sacrifices year after year.

e don't have a lasting city here, you know— ours is yet to come.

Hebrews 12:18,22-24 Now (unlike Moses) you have not come to a mountain that can be touched. . . . Rather, you have come to Mount Zion, the city of the living God, the heavenly Jerusalem and to a massive assembly of angels. . . to the general assembly and church of the firstborn recorded [in the Book of Life] in heaven, and to God, the judge of all, and to the spirits of godly men perfected [by Christ's sacrifice]. And [finally] (you've come) to Jesus, the mediator of the new Will and Testament. . . .

Philippians 3:20 We are citizens of heaven, whereby we also eagerly wait for our Saviour, the Lord Jesus Christ.

Hebrews 11:10 (Abraham) . . . was of course looking for the city Whose builder and architect is God.

I n bearing Jesus's disgrace then, let us continually praise God by sacrificing in our own lives, showing Him our thanks, rather than merely giving lip service.

Hebrews 5:8,9 . . . Although He was a Son, He suffered, and He learned obedience from these things that He suffered. He was perfected by God and became the source of everlasting salvation for all who obey Him through suffering.

I Peter 1:14,15 As *obedient* children, don't maintain the former desires which you had while ignorant, but like the Holy One (Christ) Who called you, be holy yourselves in everything you do.

Colossians 3:23-25 Whatever you do, do it from the heart like you're doing it for the Lord, rather than for men, knowing that you will receive the reward of inheritance from the Lord; it is Christ you serve. The person who does wrong things will receive the consequences of those acts without any partiality.

God is pleased when you share and do good things; don't forget to sacrifice in this way.

Hebrews 3:1,13,14 Siblings in [Christ], you were tapped for God's own purposes. . . . All day long encourage each other, day after day, so that not one of you will be hardened by sinful tricks and lies. For we are in Christ's blessings if we keep our faith to the end.

I Peter 4:10,11 Since each one of you has received a special gift from God, use it in serving each other, as good fiduciaries of the encompassing kindness of God. Whoever speaks, speak the words of God; whoever serves, do so with the strength supplied by God, so that in all things God may be glorified through Jesus Christ, to Whom belongs glory and control for all time.

Your leaders watch over your souls as if they would be called to account for your actions, so obey them and be submissive (to their leadership).

Hebrews 6:11,12 It's our desire that each one of you is as diligent as ever so you'll be full of hope until the end. So that you won't be slow in this, just imitate the faithful and patient people who inherit God's promises.

Hebrews 13:7 Think about your leaders who spoke God's word to you and imitate their faith, remembering how they died for it.

Don't cause them grief, for this won't profit you, but rather let them lead you with joy.

Pray for us (the apostles)—we have a good conscience and want to act honorably in all things.

Acts 24:16 . . . I try my best to keep a guilt-free conscience before both God and mankind.

I Thessalonians 5:25 [Dear] siblings in Christ, [please] pray for us.

Ephesians 6:19,20 Pray for me so [God] will give me the words when I open my mouth to be bold in revealing the mysteries of the true account of Christ, even while I'm in chains.

 urge you to pray, also, that I may come back to you as soon as possible.

Hebrews 13:23 Please note that our brother in Christ, Timothy, has been released (from prison). If he comes soon I will be with him and see you then.

May the One Who brought the great Shepherd of the sheep up from the dead, the God of peace, Who through the blood of Jesus our Lord

Hebrews 9:16,17 Where there is a will, the one who makes it has to die [for the contractual will to be enforced]. It's, of course, never in force while the one who made it lives, since a Will and Testament is only valid when death occurs.

Hebrews 9:28 . . . Christ, Who suffered once for the sins of many, shall appear a second time, and not that time to bear sin, but to [judge] those who eagerly wait for Him for their salvation.

Hebrews 9:15 . . . [Because of His self-sacrifice] He is the mediator of a new contract between God and man [God's new Will and Testament].

Hebrews 10:16 "This is the Will and Testament I will make with them at the close of the age, says the Lord: I will put My laws upon their heart and upon their mind I will write them."

[validated] the everlasting Will and Testament between man and God, equip you with the best tools to do His will.

Hebrews 10:36-38 You need to endure, so that when you've done God's will, you may receive that (inheritance) He promised you. "For yet in a very little while, He Who is coming will come and will not delay. My righteous One shall live by faith. But [the one who] shrinks back, my soul has no pleasure in him."

By us [being so equipped], (God) works to accomplish things that make Him happy.

Hebrews 4:3 Those of us who do believe will enter His tranquil rest—not death.

 hrough Jesus Christ, glory be to Him forever and ever. Amen.

Hebrews 4:12,13 Now the Word of God [Christ] is a living thing. It's active and sharper than any two-edged sword, piercing to the divisions of the spirit and soul and the body and its life forces; able to judge not only the thoughts, but also the intentions. All things are seen by Christ, (the One Who is the reason we're here).

 urge you to listen to what I'm asking you to do in this brief letter.

Please note that our brother in Christ, Timothy, has been released (from prison). If he comes soon I will be with him and see you then.

Tell all of your leaders and the true believers hello for me. (Our [siblings] in Christ) in Italy also say hello.

 ay the kindness and forgiveness of God be shown to you all.

Revelation 7:17 "The Lamb, at the center of the throne, shall shepherd *them*, and guide them to the springs of the waters of life, and God shall wipe every tear away from their eyes."

Revelation 22:3 There shall no longer be any curse, and the throne of God and of the Lamb shall be in it (the *holy city, new Jerusalem*), and His bond-servants shall serve Him.

Hebrews 4:16 Let's go up with confidence to God's seat of forgiveness so that we can receive mercy and kindness to help us through the tough times.

Index

of
People
Places
and
Things
in
The Bible Made Easy™: Hebrews

A

Aaron	79-81, 87, 122, 124-125, 127, 130, 177, 185, 194-195, 228, 230, 240, 255-256, 259-260, 271, 285, 290, 327, 419, 448
Abandon(ing)	147, 437, 475
Abba	136
Abel	388-389, 473
Abide (ing)	111, 196, 204, 243, 250
Abolish(ed)	63, 143, 219
Abominable	338, 349
Abraham; Abram	13, 20, 53, 65-66, 135, 167-169, 171, 174, 179, 181-182, 184, 186-189, 191-192, 199-200, 208, 235-236, 249, 280, 329, 370, 396-398, 400, 402, 404, 408-410, 414, 465, 486, 502; 135, 182, 396-398
Absolve	277
Abundant	412, 460
Accept(ed) (able)	98, 376, 488, 313, 472, 480
Adam	138, 153, 326, 329, 342-343, 364
Adultery; Adulterous	31, 264, 309
Adversaries	364
Advocate	164, 216
Afflicted	59, 141, 143, 299, 431, 494
Afraid	62, 137, 207-208, 214, 305, 310, 415, 453, 464, 491, 493
Aggressive	458
Agony	38, 136
Agreement	34, 102, 108, 196, 212, 233, 237, 242-243, 250, 301, 319
Alien(s)	167, 397, 404
Allot(ment)	71, 130, 143, 230, 297, 301, 381
Almighty	30, 205, 223, 312
Alone	118, 133
Amazement	336
Amends	23, 125, 127-128, 164, 195, 261, 275, 289, 292, 327, 342
Ananias	151
Anarchy	379
Andrew	296
Angel(s)	26, 25, 29, 30-31, 37, 38, 40, 46, 48, 50-51, 58, 65, 104, 118, 136, 141, 142, 168, 213, 224, 235, 251, 258, 266, 267, 297, 302, 309, 311, 314, 365, 375, 382, 384, 393, 409, 418, 422, 430, 440, 465-466, 471, 475, 478-479, 482-483, 486, 502
Anger; Angry	24, 26-27, 37, 65, 88, 89, 94-95, 248, 306, 312, 371, 418, 464
Annihilation	154
Anoint(ed) (ing)	25-26, 32-33, 44, 129, 138, 260, 289-291, 381, 441
Answer(ed)	47, 113, 118, 140, 152, 168, 209, 264, 296, 310, 316, 336, 382, 409, 422, 428, 455, 462, 493
Antichrist	39
Antioch	431
Apostle(s)	140, 355, 361, 375, 430-431, 471, 507

F ————————————————————————————

	359, 360, 364, 366, 372, 393, 400, 409, 428, 443, 450, 454, 469, 472, 474, 491, 495, 502, 512, 516
Light	31, 35, 150, 269, 277, 281, 304, 322, 351, 359, 365, 373, 437, 458, 481
Loathed	87
Lord; Lords	14, 18, 21, 22, 24, 26, 27, 29, 30, 32, 34, 35, 37, 38, 41, 43, 49, 50, 57, 58, 62, 64, 70, 71, 74, 76, 78-81, 83-89, 92, 93, 97, 99, 100, 102, 108, 109, 111, 112, 115, 117, 118, 120, 122, 124-127, 129-131, 134, 135, 141-143, 151-153, 157, 162, 164, 166, 168, 169, 173, 175, 177, 179, 184, 185, 191, 192, 194-196, 201, 203, 205, 207, 208, 210, 212-214, 222-223, 225, 228, 230, 233, 234, 238, 239, 241, 243, 244, 246-249, 255-257, 260, 266, 269, 273, 281, 285, 290, 291, 295-298, 300, 302, 303, 305, 306, 308, 315, 316, 318, 319, 321, 326-328, 344, 349-352, 355, 357, 359, 360, 362, 364, 365, 370, 371, 376, 377, 380, 382, 383, 393, 396, 400, 402, 408, 409, 412, 418-423, 428, 431, 436, 439, 441, 443-446, 451, 453, 455, 461, 465, 467, 469, 475, 477-479, 481, 484, 486, 491, 493, 495, 502, 503, 509; 486
Love(ed) (s) (ing)	20, 25, 27, 32, 33, 51, 93, 99, 110, 138, 148-150, 152, 161-163, 168, 207, 219, 226, 239, 248, 249, 268, 273, 275, 276, 279, 308, 324-325, 314, 332, 336, 340, 343, 360, 361, 379, 382, 409, 443, 444-446, 451, 459, 469, 479, 481, 485, 491, 492
Loyalty	352, 392
Luke	38, 43, 48, 82, 117, 136, 155, 227, 235, 294, 295, 318, 331, 338, 340, 347, 392, 429, 453, 492
Lust(s)	264, 437, 490
Lying	110, 150, 279, 314, 347, 379
M	
Magdalene	295
Magnificence	117
Magnified	53
Majesty; Majestic	273; 224, 299
Mamre	397, 486
Manasseh	199, 413
Manifested	76, 204, 201, 352
Mankind	48, 82, 212, 233, 235, 249, 250, 269, 281, 294, 302, 307, 341, 360, 394, 465, 470, 473, 485, 507
Manna	255, 339
Mark	16, 24, 28, 31, 43, 44, 47, 60, 84, 136, 204, 226, 264, 295, 305, 309, 313, 365, 392, 441, 472
Marriage; Married	489, 490; 398, 489
Martha	428
Martyrs	471
Marvel	96
Mary	141, 200, 295, 361